A LENT STUDY FOR MEN

THE
FINAL DAYS
OF JESUS

FROM SACRED HOLIDAYS

Published by Sacred Holidays. © 2017 Chris Kiser

No part of this book may be reproduced or transmitted in any form or by any means, electronic or mechanical, including photocopying and recording, or by any information storage or retrieval system, except as may be expressly permitted by Sacred Holidays or Becky Kiser. Requests for permission should be sent to hello@sacredholidays.com. This does exclude sharing visuals of the study on social media in order to share what God is teaching you with others or to help promote the book.

ISBN 978-0-9982268-5-9

Unless otherwise noted, all Scripture quotations are from the ESV Study Bible
The Holy Bible, English Standard Version® (ESV®)
Copyright © 2001 by Crossway, a publishing ministry of Good News Publishers.
All rights reserved.
ESV® Permanent Text Edition® (2016)

Cover and interior design: Megan Nicole Media (www.megannicolemedia.com)

To order additional copies of this resource:
Visit the online shop: www.sacredholidays.com/shop

To order in bulk at a discounted rate (orders over 50 studies) for churches, bookstores, ministries or non-profits, contact hello@sacredholidays.com

If you know someone who is unable to afford this study and you are unable to purchase it for him or her, please see the Discounts page under the Lent tab at www.sacredholidays.com.

Printed in the United States of America

Sacred Holidays, P.O. BOX 131476, Spring, Texas, 77381

TABLE OF CONTENTS

Hello from Chris

How this Study Works

Reflect + Commit + Fast

HELLO

"What does it mean to be Christ-like?"

Six years ago we welcomed our first baby girl into our family. Becky (my wife) and I were borderline obsessed with names. On multiple date nights, we would plop ourselves down at a bookstore surrounded with 5 or 6 name books apiece and start throwing out names that we liked. We believed that our kid's lives were designed and ordained by God for a purpose known only to Him. We wanted their names to reflect that purpose even if it seemed impossible to know what that was at the time.

Then it happened. When I came across the C's, I found my name and the meaning of it.

"Christ-like".

Ever since that day I've turned this question around in my head... over and over and over. It has led me to acknowledge some uncomfortable truths about myself where my preferences, desires and pleasures don't line up with Jesus'. It has forced me to question the purpose and meaning behind my existence and wrestle with the reality that I may not be experiencing all that He has for me while scrolling through my news feed or accomplishing seemingly insignificant things during my day.

Yet there has been fruit from this pursuit of Jesus in my own life. There is such a desire to know the Jesus of the Bible. Not the Jesus of the Sunday School I happened to attend or the geographic location I've settled in. Not the Jesus of my comfort or the Jesus that is never bothered, always in control, radiating peace that seems far from attainable. I wanted to know Him.

I want you to know Him.

This study is about that. Your identity as a man is rooted in the One who created you, who formed you in your mother's womb and who gave you a purpose and a calling and a name. What if we didn't question that purpose or calling but instead felt equipped to live it? What if we could think of Lent not as just a season of giving something up but as a season to release yourself to be known and loved and fulfilled by Him?

We're going to study towards that end. And pray towards that end. And live towards that end. Welcome to a study about Jesus' final days and the depth of His pursuits. I can't wait for us to experience this.

CHRIS KISER

HOW THIS STUDY WORKS

The format of this study is pretty simple. Each week follows a similar format and will mostly be a single page of content and a single page of three questions. This study is meant to be interactive by nature. It's not a book you sit down and read days and days at a time. It is formatted in a way that asks your heart to be engaged more than your head. It explores disciplines of reflection, solitude and silence in an effort to help you hear God's voice over my own.

You'll see I'm a fan of consistency and simplicity to remove any barriers of engagement that may exist. I don't want to overwhelm you with content or questions only to see you put the study down in week 2 because it's too much to keep up with. Think of this more as an invitation to experience a deeper relationship with God at a pace you can keep no matter what your schedule looks like for a particular day. If you have 15-20 minutes, you can do a day at a time.

Daily Charge

Discipline and reflection will be core to this study and there will be ample opportunity to dig into both almost every day of Lent. We'll begin everyday with these five prompts to put us in the right mindset to engage with Jesus and deepen our faith through study, reflection and application. The first week of the study will solely explore each of these prompts showing the importance of these disciplines. Don't skip over these as you are eager to get into the content. This study is about relationship over knowledge. Engaging with Scripture over checking a box.

PRAISE GOD. REPENT OF SIN. ASK FOR OTHERS + YOURSELF. YIELD TO GOD.

WAIT AND LISTEN.

Light Days | Sunday

These days we'll be incorporating candles to represent the light that Jesus is in our life. We'll start with all 7 candles lit and then each week we'll blow out a single candle in remembrance of His life, His death and ultimately His resurrection. Light days will hold the most original content as we'll explore ways in which we should think and walk and live when we grasp how Jesus' life brought hope (a.k.a. light) to our darkness. On Good Friday, all candles should be blown out. Then on Easter Sunday, the day Jesus rose from the dead and conquered death once and for all, we'll light all 7 candles as a visual reminder of the light He is to this world and the light we are now called to walk in.

Justice Days | Monday

Jesus didn't only teach during His life, but He discipled close followers of His as well as healed and interacted with some of society's most broken, hurting, needy people and their circumstances. These days will speak to how we can be His hands and feet in our world today. We'll talk about Justice for the Sick and Lame, the Poor, Sinners, the Hungry, the Broken Hearted and the Confused and Anxious. We're called to help those who are weak in a certain area. We also should acknowledge our weakness in these areas and reach out for help when needed. These days are about the Church being the Church in our world. We want to love God and others well.

Scripture Days | Tuesday, Thursday and Saturday

Scripture days are designed as the substance of the study. If you do nothing else, we ask you to make these days a priority. We'll take one moment from Jesus' final days, write out the Scripture with some other references where it makes sense and ask three thought provoking questions along with some short commentary where appropriate. This is essentially how we do house church at our local church each Wednesday night. We aren't seeking to simply know what the Scripture says but we're instead asking Jesus to reveal His heart, His meaning and His purpose behind His words. It is my goal for us to be in a posture where true healing and transformation can take place in our hearts as we experience His final days all over again through a different lens.

Sabbath Days | Wednesday

The Bible has much to say about being still and silent before the Lord. It also has much to say about resting from your work and taking stock of all the Lord has done in and around you. We will not be introducing any content on Sabbath days but instead will be inviting you to simply rest and renew yourself through guided questions. These days are not catch up days for when you fall behind. They are there as markers to help you acknowledge the ways He is working in your heart and for you to hear clearly from your Father how He loves you today. Lean into His rest and feel whatever burden you're carrying around be lifted.

Prayer Days | Friday

On prayer days, I'll be walking you through a practice I've done for the last couple of years on a trip I've taken with Adventures of the Heart in the mountains of Colorado. We'll pray through a guided prayer meant to steady your heart for the day. Then I'll ask a couple of questions for you to respond to in prayer. It won't be long by design, but my aim is to help you get a little more comfortable with silence than you are today and feel closer to the Lord through regular interaction with Him.

Daily Application

Each day will end the same with a single question:

How can you apply what you have heard today? (James 1:22).

The question is the same each day but your response will likely be different depending on how you're hearing God speak to you. Write down your thoughts freely as you learn to hear His voice and apply that leading to your everyday actions and words. Also it's very important to remember that His words will always align with Scripture. Our feelings don't always. Be careful to listen to the right voice.

REFLECT + COMMIT + FAST

REFLECT

I'm a big advocate for planning and executing on a plan. Getting time alone to prepare for a week and seeing your schedule instead of responding to everyone else's schedule is necessary if you want to avoid getting caught up in an endless cycle of activity. So below are some prompts that will allow you to reflect on what brought you to this place and help clarify what you'd like to take away from this study when you celebrate Christ's resurrection on Easter Sunday.

Do the hard work of reflection and reap the benefits of clarity and purpose during your study times.

▶ *How would you describe your relationship with the Lord right now? Be honest. No one will see this but you.*

▶ *How often do you spend focused time with Him—not rushed or on-the-go time, but still and focused time with Him?*

▶ *What does studying the Word look like for you?*

▶ *What does prayer look like for you?*

▶ How have the holidays affected your spiritual walk in the past?

▶ Last Easter, did you feel closer to the Lord because of how you were pursuing Him?

▶ Why did you pick up this Lent Bible study?

▶ What do you hope to get out of it?

COMMIT

Our commitments require our full heart to be engaged if they're ever going to become a reality. How about during this study we stop thinking all of this should come easy and that we should be more disciplined than we really are. This is hard work! It requires planning and faith and belief to keep your focus on Christ during this season. Our enemy would like nothing more than to keep you occupied in other priorities. Knowing it won't be easy is half the battle.

Commit this time to Him. You are worth it. He is worth it.

I don't want to set the bar low for us. What if you really could meet with Him and learn to hear His voice? What if your heart was changed throughout the study so that when Easter Sunday came you were truly thankful for Jesus' life and gift of eternity to you? It can happen.

Last, can I encourage you to pursue Him with a singular focus? There is Scripture all throughout this study and lessons that can serve as content during your time with the Lord. If you've committed to this and 2 other things, your attention will be divided. I would encourage you to do one study so that it gets your full attention.

▶ *How will you make time to do your Bible study each day?*

• *Write down when and where you will do your Bible study, then set an alarm on your phone to go off each day at the time listed above. Initial below once you've set your alarm (morning, afternoon or night).*

What obstacles will try to prevent you from making this time a reality? List each one out below. Write out your action plan to get past them.

OBSTACLES	WHAT CAN YOU DO ABOUT IT?

Is there anything that might be helpful to avoid (or fast from) this Easter in order to be more fully or freely engaged? This is optional, and not at all required. I find it helpful in various seasons to pull away from something completely or conditionally (once I've connected with Christ that day) in order that I might be more fully engaged with my time in His Word. Examples: social media, TV/Netflix, mindless Internet browsing, etc.

- *Write out a prayer to the Lord committing this study to Him. Make your promise of how you will meet with Him. Ask Him to help you keep that.*

Share this with someone(s) and write his or her name(s) below. We do better in life when we live in community. Snap a pic of these pages and share them with a friend, or show them to a family member, or even share them on social media. The accountability will be good.

And done. So proud of you. We value your time and are praying for God to move powerfully in your life as a result. Thank you for trusting us and trusting Him with your time. Tomorrow we begin a study that has been labored over, prayed over and fought for. I can't wait for you to experience Him.

FAST

"Yet even now," declares the Lord, "return to me with all your heart, with fasting, with weeping, and with mourning; and rend your hearts and not your garments."

Return to the Lord your God, for he is gracious and merciful, slow to anger, and abounding in steadfast love;"

Joel 2:12-13a (ESV)

Fasting and prayer are linked throughout Scripture. Whether fasting is talked about to deepen our worship of the Lord, to eliminate food to free up time to intercede for others or to simply serve as a symbolic gesture to say our faith and trust is in the Lord to sustain us over our normal means, one thing is consistent. Fasting is purposeful and is a discipline practiced by Jesus as well as His disciples to sacrifice their immediate well-being for a higher purpose and calling.

It's your choice what you will fast from during these days of Lent. Some fast from food during certain hours while others will fast from something that currently has a stronghold on their life. The only thing I want to be clear on is that fasting is the willful abstaining from something in exchange for deeper connection with the Lord. Simply not eating or not getting on Facebook for 40 days without engaging Jesus during that time will not lead you into a deeper appreciation or dependence on Him.

My only encouragement here is that you prayerfully identify what you should fast from and make a plan for ways that you will engage with Jesus during those gaps of time. There are plenty of Scriptures to look at as well if you search for fasting that will help clarify the heart and purpose behind it as well.

This is a discipline that our western culture doesn't engage in regularly and I would easily be a part of that stereotype. This will take a certain level of faith just because we can't rely on our familiarity or comfort to get us through this commitment.

▶ *What will you fast from this Lent season?*

▶ *What will you do in these gaps of time to deepen your relationship with the Lord?*

WEEK ONE

PRAISE GOD

PRAISE GOD. REPENT OF SIN. ASK FOR OTHERS + YOURSELF. YIELD TO GOD. WAIT AND LISTEN.

Praise is such a lost art to some of us.

Think about a time where you couldn't wait to express your thanks or love or respect towards someone. It wasn't something you had to do, but instead it was a pleasure to take part in making much of someone else.

This is the praise we're striving for in our appreciation and thanks toward God.

▶ *Can you remember the look on a person's face that you genuinely praised? Write about it below.*

Each day of this study is going to begin with the exact same prompt. We'll explore each aspect of this prompt for the next four days because I don't want us to miss out on the fruit this will bring.

Lent is historically marked as a season of prayer and repentance. It's introspective and holds riches in both knowledge and action that we can't find other places. Growing up I had thought it was only for certain people to experience, but I've since been convinced the tradition and ritual behind it has so much life in it that we can't afford the deception any longer.

This is for all of us. Young believer or experienced. Find your faith by taking 10 minutes to dwell on where God has moved you to praise Him. Relive the celebrations that you have experienced and also the times where your heart responded to Him in the midst of unspeakable pain. See His love towards you by discovering all over again His presence in the midst of your life.

He is a personal God, worthy of and enjoying our praise for Him. Let's acknowledge Him today.

- Write out a few celebrations that you've experienced that have moved you to praise the Lord for who He is and for how He was moving.

▶ Write out a couple of moments where you praised Him in the midst of loss, pain, confusion, or the empty feeling of inadequacy. Where did He comfort you the most?

▶ Romans 8:31 says, "... If God is for us, who can be against us?" Write out verse 32 below. What does this communicate about God's heart towards us?

⟩ **DOER OF THE WORD** ⟨

How can you apply what you have heard today? (James 1:22)

REPENTANCE + JUSTICE

PRAISE GOD. REPENT OF SIN. ASK FOR OTHERS + YOURSELF. YIELD TO GOD. WAIT AND LISTEN.

Today is Ash Wednesday. It's a day that gives meaning to repentance.

Do you make it a habit to consider the context of the story that you're living in? Often times, without understanding the origin or historical meaning of certain events or circumstances, we're left either performing rituals or forming habits devoid of the life they were meant to lead us into or, worse yet, end up settling for a story far less significant than what God had intended. Not being obedient to Him or His heart towards us because we don't place priority on it is a mistake. Repentance, I believe, is a discipline that we explore far less frequently than we ought.

"Repent, and believe in the Gospel."

Repentance is often viewed through the lens of giving something up. For 40 days, Jesus spent time in the desert fasting and endured the relentless temptation of Satan. He gave up what could sustain Him on Earth, yet pursued His Father and relied on Him and His word to give Him the strength to resist.

Repentance is an action towards life, not an act of deprivation.

It's a tradition carried out to cleanse our hearts from distraction and from our simplistic view of satisfaction. He has far more in store for us than what we settle for on a regular basis. I'm preaching to myself with this truth.

When you read this daily, search your heart and discover your true beliefs. Are you believing lies that you need to abandon? Do you believe that He came to Earth and lived a life of sacrifice, of relationship and of fulfillment all so that you could spend your time on Earth growing into the person He created you to be? All for a final reward of an eternity spent with the One who sustains and who offers true life?

Are you believing God and experiencing His pursuit of your heart? Does believing the gospel change your attitude towards yourself or the way you talk to those closest to you?

He is calling us to see the bigger picture of repentance. We beg you Lord, do a work in our hearts and move us to experience the love You have for us.

- Ask the Lord what He is calling you to repent from. Wait and listen. Write down below what you hear Him saying to you.

▶ What does believing the gospel look like? Explore this question and write down any thoughts you have.

▶ Ashes represent a deep sorrow for our own sins or inexpressible grief and sometimes loss. What do they represent for you? What are you grieving? Where have you experienced loss? Let it focus your thoughts on Him.

DO JUSTICE

In staying with the theme of repentance towards something, we will have a special focus on Monday's towards **doing justice**.

- Write out Micah 6:8 and then circle the three things we should do.

The Message translates this passage, "But he's already made it plain how to live, what to do, what God is looking for in men and women. It's quite simple: Do what is fair and just to your neighbor, be compassionate and loyal in your love, And don't take yourself too seriously— take God seriously."

As we are actively praising God, repenting of our sin and believing the gospel, we also want to be Christ-like in our actions towards ourselves and others. This can look very different for each of us, but the important thing to grasp is God's heart towards justice in our world and your part in it.

Make no mistake. This involves you. Gone are the days where we watch passively as God engages the hearts of men around you but seemingly doesn't appeal to you in the same way. Remember, He is a creator God and He created you unique and for a purpose. That purpose can be discovered in these days. You have a part in this story and a role in the justice that God brings to our world.

Read these verses and write what they teach you about justice.

• **Proverbs 21:15**

• **Psalm 37:27-29**

• **Isaiah 1:17**

• **Zechariah 7:9-10**

• **Jeremiah 22:3**

This calling can feel quite daunting. Yet, seen in its proper context, it should bring a feeling of freedom and adventure. The Bible has much to say about Jesus' role in bringing justice to our lives.

- *Write out Isaiah 42:1*

Behold my servant, whom I uphold, my chosen, in whom my soul delights; I have put my Spirit upon him; he will bring forth justice to the nations

Read on past this verse all the way to verse 9. He promises to keep us, to open eyes that are blind, to restore prisoners who sit in darkness out into a light that cleanses their sins. He will not be discouraged in the work and will not declare defeat over a seemingly hopeless cause.

▶ *What feelings are stirred up in you as you read God's heart towards justice? Are you in need of justice yourself or aware of another's need?*

DOER OF THE WORD

How can you apply what you have heard today? (James 1:22)

ASK FOR YOURSELF AND OTHERS

PRAISE GOD. REPENT OF SIN. ASK FOR OTHERS + YOURSELF.
YIELD TO GOD. WAIT AND LISTEN.

This invitation to ask should be taken literally and practiced often. Making petitions to God or simply speaking or writing out loud your thoughts to Him allows you to take part in the answer that God will give you for each specific thing. Jesus tells us to ask and gives us a glimpse of what might happen if we believe Him enough to do it.

- **Write out Matthew 7:7-8, 11**

While I was at Purdue, I used to ask all kinds of questions to God in my head as I was working my way through the Bible for the first time. I grew up in a home where questions were always respected. They were encouraged. So this came naturally to me that when I ran into something I didn't know or didn't understand, I would simply ask.

▶ **What are one or two questions that you've asked of God. Did you get a response?**

Some of my questions would be answered through a story in the Bible. I would wonder what different parts of the culture thought about Jesus at the time and would get a good idea by reading. I would ask Him about relationships or loneliness and read examples of both. My requests turned into conversations and I started seeing parallels between relationships here and with Him.

I started my asking in prayer by referring to God as God. "Dear God..." were the words that began so many of my prayers. It slowly turned to "Father..." Formalities gave way to language that comes from being known.

Ask your Father in Heaven about what is on your heart. Beg Him to make your desires come alive in due time. Crave the process of learning from your Creator God and expect an answer. Let's begin our days by following through on the instruction and figuring out why it was so important to God to include it in His Holy Bible.

- **Read Luke 8:40-56 and write what you've learned about asking God.**

▶ **What do you take away from the father's plea with Jesus for his daughter?**

- **Write down one or two requests that you've been praying for many years. Keep asking until you feel the Lord give you an answer. Nothing is too small or too big.**

> **DOER OF THE WORD**

How can you apply what you have heard today? (James 1:22)

YIELD TO GOD

PRAISE GOD. REPENT OF SIN. ASK FOR OTHERS + YOURSELF. YIELD TO GOD. WAIT AND LISTEN.

For the last two years I've taken a 5 day trip to the mountains in Colorado with a group of about 60 guys. The retreat is both restful and exhausting as each day is filled with a mix of Bible teaching, hours of focused journaling, down time, ping pong games, a jeep excursion and the building of deep relationships. It's a week where you feel Jesus coming after your heart and redeeming your heart, not only for the adventure you're attempting to live today but for the legacy you'll set for those that come after you.

Each day there are times set aside where you're given questions to journal through. You're given anywhere from an hour to two hours or longer and told very explicit instructions.

"Don't come back until you've heard from the Lord on these questions."

• **Write briefly about a time where you felt invited into a larger story.**

I settled under a large birch tree and sat in complete silence for what seemed like an eternity. What was I even doing here? I've never heard God's voice that I can recall. The rule follower in me was getting nervous that I may not see the camp any time soon.

So I waited. Slowly the silence became comfortable. The wind started blowing and then stopped instantly. Without hesitation, I started writing word for word what came to mind without self checking.

To yield is another way of saying to give over.

▶ **What expectations have you given over to God and yielded to His purposes or calling beyond what you could presently understand?**

Yielding to God daily in this study is simply surrendering to what He has in store for you to experience. It isn't forcing yourself to read in order to check off a list or to box God into a corner and expecting Him to work in ways that only you're comfortable with. It is trusting His will over your own and actively, with your actions, saying yes. This is where your belief will be tested. This is also the area where you will see, feel and possibly hear Him moving as your posture becomes one of receiving from Him.

• **Write out Ephesians 5:1-2**

▶ **Where have you been able to yield to God's will without hesitation?**

▶ **Where have you had a difficult time yielding to God or others? What are the biggest obstacles you experience when you try to give over your expectations?**

> **DOER OF THE WORD** <

How can you apply what you have heard today? (James 1:22)

SABBATH: WAIT AND LISTEN

PRAISE GOD. REPENT OF SIN. ASK FOR OTHERS + YOURSELF.
YIELD TO GOD. WAIT AND LISTEN.

The Bible has much to say about waiting and listening. Our culture, on the other hand, has drifted further and further away from this in our world of smart devices and 24/7 connectivity.

Resting, solitude and silence don't come easy. Let's begin with a good amount of verses to help teach us the wisdom behind these disciplines and let's listen for the commands to come out of Scripture to actually take a Sabbath.

Read the following verses and write out what they teach you about Sabbath, waiting, silence and listening:

• **Genesis 2:3**

• **Exodus 20:8-11**

• **Mark 2:27**

• **Mark 1:35**

• **Luke 5:15-16**

- Luke 6:12-13

- Matthew 14:13

- Matthew 14:23

We will implement this into our study. There will be a whole day marked for rest and, just as important, restoration. How you answer the following questions will help decide how you spend your Sabbath days of rest.

▶ **What is most restful (recharging) for you?**

▶ **What helps you hear from God best?**

Remember to refer back to this page during the weekly Sabbath days and put this plan into practice.

DOER OF THE WORD

How can you apply what you have heard today? (James 1:22)

WEEK TWO

WALK IN THE LIGHT

Matthew 21, Mark 11, Luke 19, John 12

PRAISE GOD. REPENT OF SIN. ASK FOR OTHERS + YOURSELF.
YIELD TO GOD. WAIT AND LISTEN.

I have come into the world as light, so that whoever believes in me may not remain in darkness.

John 12:46 ESV

As you read the beginning parts of the chapters listed above, notice the details of each account and ask the Lord to take you to that moment. The account in Matthew 21:10 excites my imagination when it says, "The whole city was stirred up."

▶ *When was the last time you were stirred up because of Jesus' presence?*

Many people in town that day weren't anticipating Jesus' arrival. They had no idea who was coming or knowledge of the prophecies in Zechariah 9:9 and Isaiah 62:11 that Jesus was fulfilling by arriving into the city. It was the reaction of the people that sparked the interest of the entire city.

Those that knew Him, or at least knew of Him because of stories that were shared didn't keep the news to themselves. They identified Jesus as the prophet from Nazareth, threw their cloaks on the ground as a symbol of their submission to their coming King and waved palm branches as a sign of victory. Those in power were restless and felt their influence slipping. All the while Jesus was introducing us to a new way of life.

Light, as is talked about in conjunction with Jesus, represented both knowledge and purity. What a harsh yet freeing reality it was to them and is to us as we set our attention on the Savior of the world. He came to represent everything we couldn't possibly be for ourselves. All knowing? Not a chance. We can't remember enough or learn fast enough. Pure? Please. My thoughts aren't His thoughts shortly after I wake up in the morning.

BLOW OUT ONE CANDLE

(YOU SHOULD HAVE 6 LIT)

Yet we're afforded the opportunity to worship without hesitation or reservation, abandoning all politeness and appearance because now we have an Advocate who is for us, who will lay down His very life and conquer sin in order for us to walk as children of the Light.

- *Write out 1 John 1:5-9.*

▶ *What set Jesus apart in the way He arrived in Jerusalem? Why were so many stirred up?*

▶ *If you lived at this time, who would you be in the story? One of the worshippers, one of the people who didn't know Jesus was coming, or one of the religious leaders who feared Jesus' purpose and influence would ruin all that they had worked towards?*

DOER OF THE WORD

How can you apply what you have heard today? (James 1:22)

JUSTICE: THE SICK AND LAME

PRAISE GOD. REPENT OF SIN. ASK FOR OTHERS + YOURSELF.
YIELD TO GOD. WAIT AND LISTEN.

On every "Justice" day, I want to start the same way as we started last week. By the end of this study, hopefully the message behind this verse brings meaning and purpose in your actions towards yourself and others.

• *Write out Micah 6:8 and then circle the three things we should do.*

The Message translates this passage, *"But he's already made it plain how to live, what to do, what God is looking for in men and women. It's quite simple: Do what is fair and just to your neighbor, be compassionate and loyal in your love, And don't take yourself too seriously— take God seriously."*

First, let's look at this topic internally. Where do you, <insert name here>, identify with the sick and the lame? Justice is not about serving only. It's absolutely not about an "us vs. them" mentality. If these types of barriers exist in any way today or if we have a desire to serve simply out of duty or obligation, I want to connect with God's heart and see if He can't bring healing to our brokenness.

▶ *Write out Isaiah 42:1. What power is in you to bring forth justice to the nations and where does it come from?*

Jesus, we ask today that you would bring healing to our sickness. For some of us, that's physical sickness, chronic pain, a terminal diagnosis or illness that affects not only us but those around us. We believe you for healing and for wholeness and where we don't, help our unbelief. Lord, for us that are lame, that aren't mobile or bedridden against our will, we ask for healing. We ask for perspective to help us understand what you might do through this debilitating state. We need hope today. Let us see your hand in this suffering and help us find comfort in your own. We pray these things in Jesus' name. Amen.

Next, let's take this heart to those around us.

▶ *Who are people you know that are dealing with sickness or lameness of some sort? Write their names or initials below.*

If you were in their shoes today, how might someone meet that need that you have in a deep and meaningful way? Sometimes words or letting them know that they were on your mind today is the best medicine they could receive for the day. Use technology for their benefit today by calling, texting, emailing or offering to Face Time out of the blue to say a quick hello. Bring a meal, offer to watch their kids or run a quick errand that may be weighing on them. There are no qualifications for being helpful. You don't have to have a certain title, live in a certain city or have a certain amount of money in your bank account. The Holy Spirit has equipped you to bring justice into this world so our only task is to ask how and be obedient.

I remember clearly the last days we had with my Nana in hospice as we watched her transfer from this life to the next. Being by her bedside brought us closer together as a family. So we decided to tell her that. My Paw Paw brought some letters up to hospice and we would read them one by one. We laughed at the ridiculousness of my Paw Paw and his crazy ideas on how to save money and satisfy Nana's urge to shop. We saw their heart for serving missionary friends while on an expat assignment overseas. We heard of their desires to have a family. In all we celebrated her, we talked to her, we cried next to her and we said our final goodbyes with full hearts.

It was where we discovered we could find beauty and feel deep pain at the same time. Don't be afraid to step into someone else's suffering. Even if you can't relate, even if you're the picture of health or don't get headaches, take a step towards loving someone where they're at.

Care for them. Love them. Provide for them. Offer to carry a burden that may be too heavy for them today. It could bring temporary relief to a very long fight.

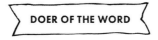

DOER OF THE WORD

In light of what you've written, read and thought about, what is one thing you can do today to take care of the sick and the lame? (James 1:22)

FAITH AND FRUIT

Matthew 21, Mark 11

PRAISE GOD. REPENT OF SIN. ASK FOR OTHERS + YOURSELF.
YIELD TO GOD. WAIT AND LISTEN.

¹⁸*In the morning, as he was returning to the city, he became hungry. ¹⁹And seeing a fig tree by the wayside, he went to it and found nothing on it but only leaves. And he said to it, "May no fruit ever come from you again!" And the fig tree withered at once.*

²⁰*When the disciples saw it, they marveled, saying, "How did the fig tree wither at once?" ²¹And Jesus answered them, "Truly, I say to you, if you have faith and do not doubt, you will not only do what has been done to the fig tree, but even if you say to this mountain, 'Be taken up and thrown into the sea,' it will happen. ²²And whatever you ask in prayer, you will receive, if you have faith."*

Matthew 21:18-22 ESV

The symbolism behind this passage is that when a fig tree started showing its leaves, fruit was right around the corner. When Jesus saw the leaves, the tree gave off the appearance as if it was going to yield fruit which would sustain and nourish. Instead, the tree didn't in fact produce any fruit at all, rendering it useless.

Jesus responding to the tree in this way didn't prevent the tree from producing fruit. It only confirmed what was already true.

Viewed in the context of our own lives, appearance has very little value in the Kingdom of God. Fruit, on the other hand, is useful to a broken and dying world when it introduces us to Jesus, our source of sustainment and nourishment. Faith is the vehicle where our desires of influence become reality.

Additional Reading: Galatians 5:16-24, Mark 11:12-14; 20-26

• Write out 3 appearances that are easy for you to hide behind.

▶ What fruit is expected to be evident in our lives? Are they all outward expressions of our faith or internal as well? (review Galatians 5:16-24)

• Identify a limiting belief you have when reading this passage. Actually telling a mountain to move and it moving is one for me personally. Ask Jesus for faith that would speak authoritatively to this limiting belief. Write your prayer out below.

DOER OF THE WORD

How can you apply what you have heard today? (James 1:22)

SABBATH: REST AND RENEW

PRAISE GOD. REPENT OF SIN. ASK FOR OTHERS + YOURSELF. YIELD TO GOD. WAIT AND LISTEN.

Welcome to Sabbath. Today is a day of rest, reflection and restoration. I encourage you to find some quiet in your day today, get alone, pray and recharge. We practice this as followers of Jesus, emulating His ways and getting alone to rest.

After [Jesus] had dismissed [the crowds], he went up on a mountainside by himself to pray. When evening came, he was [still] there alone."

Matthew 14:23 ESV

Very early in the morning, while it was still dark, Jesus got up, left the house and went off to a solitary place, where he prayed.

Mark 1:35 ESV

Refer back to the first week's entry on Sabbath to remind yourself of the things you identified as most restful to you as well as what is helpful for you when trying to hear from God. Choose today how you'll implement one or more of these suggestions. Pay attention here to how God wired you to respond to Him. It may be unique to how others experience Him. It may be very similar. The goal is not to have a relationship with Jesus like someone else does. Learn to see your unique makeup as what leads you into deeper relationship and connection. Explore that today.

Below are some questions to ponder and respond to in order to help process what the Lord has been doing in your heart. Don't worry about looking up what you've written down in prior days and repeating those answers here. Really seek the Lord and ask Him the following:

▶ *What is one truth that has stayed with me from last week?*

▶ *How would you have me apply that one truth or one lesson for this coming week?*

▶ *What do you think of me? What do you think of my heart?*

Come back and journal here about your day before you go to sleep.

▶ *What did you learn about God on your Sabbath?*

▶ *What did you learn about yourself?*

▶ *What do you need to do or not do next time to make for a more holy Sabbath?*

▶ *Anything else you learned or realized or noticed today?*

DOER OF THE WORD

How can you apply what you have heard today? (James 1:22)

GET ANGRY AND MAKE SPACE

Matthew 21, Mark 11, Luke 19

PRAISE GOD. REPENT OF SIN. ASK FOR OTHERS + YOURSELF.
YIELD TO GOD. WAIT AND LISTEN.

[15]And they came to Jerusalem. And he entered the temple and began to drive out those who sold and those who bought in the temple, and he overturned the tables of the money-changers and the seats of those who sold pigeons. [16]And he would not allow anyone to carry anything through the temple. [17]And he was teaching them and saying to them, "Is it not written, 'My house shall be called a house of prayer for all the nations'? But you have made it a den of robbers." [18]And the chief priests and the scribes heard it and were seeking a way to destroy him, for they feared him, because all the crowd was astonished at his teaching.

Mark 11:15-18 ESV

Additional Reading: Ephesians 4:26-27, Matthew 21:12-17, Luke 19:41-48

▶ Read Luke 19:41-48. What was Jesus weeping over before He cleansed the temple? Were the two events related?

▶ Other than the people's reaction, the scribes and Pharisees were afraid of the Roman response to the Israelites rising up against them. What is Jesus exposing about their motivations by His actions in the temple?

• In Matthew's account, it says "the blind and the lame came to him in the temple, and he healed them." Write out Psalm 8:2 and Matthew 21:17 and see how their response was a fulfillment of prophecy to the scribes and Pharisees.

> DOER OF THE WORD <

How can you apply what you have heard today? (James 1:22)

PRAYER: ENGAGE AND ENJOY

PRAISE GOD. REPENT OF SIN. ASK FOR OTHERS + YOURSELF.
YIELD TO GOD. WAIT AND LISTEN.

Today will be all about prayer. Prayer can take on many forms, but at its heart it is connecting with the heart of God through praising, asking, repenting and responding to His will for your life. It can be done while on your knees in a worshipful posture with your head down, while walking/running down the street, through singing with arms raised or through quiet solitude alone. So challenge yourself during these days to pray in different ways to explore the depths of your relationship with the Lord.

If the questions below are helpful for you, please use them as a guide during this time today. If you feel strongly led to engage with God in a different way that's more meaningful or personal this week, please use this time for that. While the questions and ways of praying will be the same each week, I can guarantee the actual words used, words received from God, thoughts and experiences of forgiveness, love, confusion, pain, etc. will be very different from week to week. Use the truths that you've learned in your study time and lean on the Scripture and promises that have been discovered.

Engage your heart. Enjoy the process and connection with your Creator.

- *Jesus, I want to glorify and praise you today for...*

- *This week I've felt compelled to go deeper in this area:*_____
- ▶ *I pray today that you would speak to me concerning my area of deepest need. What would you have to say to me today?*

- Lord, this week I want to confess to you where I've been most convicted. Write below where you feel God challenging you the most. This will be hard but fight for your heart in this process and be honest about where He is gently but firmly bringing His purposes to light in your life. Repent from sin. Embrace freedom in Christ.

- Jesus teaches us to long for heaven. His life was a piece of heaven coming down to Earth for us. Ask Him for His will to be done on Earth as it is in heaven. Pray for His kingdom to come to Earth and write your prayer and/or response below.

> DOER OF THE WORD <

How can you apply what you have heard today? (James 1:22)

SONS AND TENANTS

Matthew 21-22, Mark 12, Luke 20

PRAISE GOD. REPENT OF SIN. ASK FOR OTHERS + YOURSELF.
YIELD TO GOD. WAIT AND LISTEN.

"What do you think? A man had two sons. And he went to the first and said, 'Son, go and work in the vineyard today.' And he answered, 'I will not,' but afterward he changed his mind and went. And he went to the other son and said the same. And he answered, 'I go, sir,' but did not go. Which of the two did the will of his father?" They said, "The first." Jesus said to them, "Truly, I say to you, the tax collectors and the prostitutes go into the kingdom of God before you. For John came to you in the way of righteousness, and you did not believe him, but the tax collectors and the prostitutes believed him. And even when you saw it, you did not afterward change your minds and believe him."

Matthew 21:28-32 ESV

"And he began to tell the people this parable: "A man planted a vineyard and let it out to tenants and went into another country for a long while. When the time came, he sent a servant to the tenants, so that they would give him some of the fruit of the vineyard. But the tenants beat him and sent him away empty-handed. And he sent another servant. But they also beat and treated him shamefully, and sent him away empty-handed. And he sent yet a third. This one also they wounded and cast out. Then the owner of the vineyard said, 'What shall I do? I will send my beloved son; perhaps they will respect him.' But when the tenants saw him, they said to themselves, 'This is the heir. Let us kill him, so that the inheritance may be ours.' And they threw him out of the vineyard and killed him. What then will the owner of the vineyard do to them? He will come and destroy those tenants and give the vineyard to others." When they heard this, they said, "Surely not!" But he looked directly at them and said, "What then is this that is written: "'The stone that the builders rejected has become the cornerstone'? Everyone who falls on that stone will be broken to pieces, and when it falls on anyone, it will crush him."

Luke 20:9-18 ESV

Additional Reading: Matthew 21:33-46, Mark 12:1-12, James 1:14-17

- Read James 2:14-17 and look back at Matthew 21:28-32. Write the common message that Jesus is communicating in these two passages.

▶ When Jesus asked the people what would happen to the tenants when the owner of the vineyard returned for his fruit, what was their response? What was their reaction once they realized Jesus was talking about them as the tenants?

▶ Jesus' analogy of the vineyard is in fact a prophecy towards Jesus' opponents stating that the kingdom would be taken away from Israel and given to those who are producing fruit. How does this analogy speak to you today? Are you more aligned with Jesus' opponents or those producing fruit in your life today?

> **DOER OF THE WORD** <

How can you apply what you have heard today? (James 1:22)

WEEK THREE

NO FEAR IN THE LIGHT

Psalm 27:1, Psalm 56:8-13

PRAISE GOD. REPENT OF SIN. ASK FOR OTHERS + YOURSELF. YIELD TO GOD. WAIT AND LISTEN.

When is the last time you were genuinely afraid of being in the dark? The crazy thing about being in dark places is that the orientation, hand/eye coordination, and your natural instincts that you rely on is taken away from you almost instantly. One of your greatest strengths is almost instantly turned into a weakness. A personal example from my life, which is still so vivid in my memory, should help illustrate the point.

A few weeks before Becky (my wife) and I were to be married, I was living in what would become our house by myself. We had decided that when we ordered our bed that we would wait until we got back from our honeymoon to sleep in it together. So for about a month I slept in our guest bedroom on a bed that was borderline too small for me.

One night I distinctly remember being dead asleep and the next second leaping out of bed in the middle of the night. No lights, no sounds, nothing. I just remember being scared. I turned quickly one way and then the other and suddenly felt something brush my back! Without thinking, I whirled around to the other side and felt it again. Now the adrenaline was pumping. I was ready to fight as I clearly had no other options at this point.

There was only one problem. Every time I turned around to confront my attacker there wasn't anybody there. Baffled after about 10 seconds of this, I stopped and tried to figure out what was happening. Everything on my body felt fine, except for my left arm. It was missing. I looked down and touched it and realized I felt nothing. My deep sleep had transferred solely to my left arm. My attacker had finally been discovered.

▶ *Turn off all the lights or imagine yourself in a dark place. Which senses do you/would you miss the most?*

BLOW OUT ONE CANDLE

(YOU SHOULD HAVE 5 LIT)

Isn't it like us to live our daily lives thinking that our strengths will be enough? How quickly we can be reminded of our limitations when life interferes. There is a time and a place to flee from darkness, to run and escape certain situations. Yet when we can't physically escape, when darkness seems to consume us or hope isn't as easily accessible, we can run to God's word for the strength we so desperately need.

> "The Lord is my light and my salvation; whom shall I fear? The Lord is the stronghold of my life; of whom shall I be afraid?"

Psalms 27:1 ESV

What would happen if you learned the trick of embracing Jesus' light in the midst of your darkness. This can easily be in the physical realm and can become a mantra of sorts.

Jesus, you're my light and my salvation. Show me where You're working in this.

In the midst of confusion, of unmet expectations, or unspeakable personal pain, speak this verse over yourself and preach to your heart.

Jesus, you're the stronghold of my life.

It says here in the presence of the Lord, fear should not be a prevailing emotion. However, I find it fascinating that it doesn't dismiss it or act like it doesn't exist. It addresses fear head on. It puts it in its proper place. Should the light of Jesus prevail over fear? Yes. Should the Lord have a stronghold over your life that is more powerful than the feeling of being afraid? *Absolutely.*

Let these verses encourage you in your walk with the Lord. If it's the first time you're reading them in this context, let the words pour over your soul. Rest in them. Spend time with them. Recognize that any form of darkness experienced in your life should bring you back to the idea that the Lord is light. Understand deep in your heart that you serve a God who empathizes with you, who is for you, who is making all things new so that you can experience the fullness of His presence and grace.

The absence of Jesus would bring forth emotions of fear.

The presence of Him reduces fear to a simple, powerless feeling.

"You have kept count of my tossings; put my tears in your bottle. Are they not in your book? Then my enemies will turn back in the day when I call. This I know, that God is for me. In God, whose word I praise, in the Lord, whose word I praise, in God I trust; I shall not be afraid. What can man do to me? I must perform my vows to you, O God; I will render thank offerings to you. For you have delivered my soul from death, yes, my feet from falling, that I may walk before God in the light of life."

Psalms 56:8-13 ESV

▶ What do these verses stir in you as you read them?

> **DOER OF THE WORD**

How can you apply what you have heard today? (James 1:22)

JUSTICE: THE POOR

PRAISE GOD. REPENT OF SIN. ASK FOR OTHERS + YOURSELF.
YIELD TO GOD. WAIT AND LISTEN.

• *Write out Micah 6:8 and then circle the three things we should do.*

The Message translates this passage, "But he's already made it plain how to live, what to do, what God is looking for in men and women. It's quite simple: Do what is fair and just to your neighbor, be compassionate and loyal in your love, And don't take yourself too seriously— take God seriously."

First, let's look at this topic internally. Where do you, <insert name here>, identify with the poor? Justice is not about serving only. It's absolutely not about an "us vs. them" mentality. If these types of barriers exist in any way today or if we have a desire to serve simply out of duty or obligation, I want to connect with God's heart and see if He can't bring healing to our brokenness.

▶ *In what ways are you poor today? List out 2 or 3 things that come to mind.*

Jesus, we ask today that You would hear us. We identify with the poor in the ways we listed above and know that You are close to us. I ask that You would help us see the purpose behind our current state. Jesus, let us not be victims today but let us feel Your presence and understand we are loved and taken care of because of You, who we know. Let us accept that as richness today. We pray for opportunity to live out our callings and support ourselves and our families through hard work. Where we're poor in spirit, feel inadequate or not worthy, I pray Jesus that our identity would be secure in You and You would teach us our heritage where we would remember on the lowest of days. Where we are lacking I pray for abundant grace in seeing where we are not. I pray you would encourage our faith in You today through provision or understanding. We pray these things in Jesus' name. Amen.

Next, let's take this heart to those around us.

▶ *Who are people you know that are poor? Write their names or initials below.*

Today, what can you do to impact someone's life around you where they would feel the Lord's closeness? Could you provide fresh clothes, towels, a meal, a bed, or a toy to someone in need? Becky and I talked to a homeless man in Seattle for about 30 minutes one day over coffee. You know what he taught us about being poor? He taught us to both ask and accept with a thankful heart. He stood on the street daily, at the same spot, asking if anyone had money so he could pay for his visit to the doctor. He had cancer. He had a need and was trying to meet the need in the only way he knew how.

What we saw that day changed me. He had people come up to him that obviously had seen him before on their way to work. One man gave him a bear hug when he saw him and they talked as if they were long lost brothers. He offered to get him coffee or breakfast but he declined as those needs had already been met by someone else. Others walked by him without making eye contact and went on their way.

We asked, "Do you get offended when people don't offer you money?" He seemed so confused. "Oh no." he said. "I know they work hard for their money and I know they have all kinds of things to take care of. I understand it." We ended up giving him what little we had in cash that day and it almost brought tears to his eyes. Not of sadness that he wasn't going to be able to pay the whole doctor bill, but of gladness because he was closer than he was before. His reaction, his face was joy personified. That was light. He knew God had taken care of a need that day and felt his worries were resting with the One who knew how to handle them. He was not limited by money nor enabled by it.

DOER OF THE WORD

In light of what you've written, read and thought about, what is one thing you can do today to take care of the poor? (James 1:22)

PAY TAXES AND WIDOW'S OFFERING

PRAISE GOD. REPENT OF SIN. ASK FOR OTHERS + YOURSELF.
YIELD TO GOD. WAIT AND LISTEN.

"And they sent to him some of the Pharisees and some of the Herodians, to trap him in his talk. And they came and said to him, "Teacher, we know that you are true and do not care about anyone's opinion. For you are not swayed by appearances, but truly teach the way of God. Is it lawful to pay taxes to Caesar, or not? Should we pay them, or should we not?" But, knowing their hypocrisy, he said to them, "Why put me to the test? Bring me a denarius and let me look at it." And they brought one. And he said to them, "Whose likeness and inscription is this?" They said to him, "Caesar's." Jesus said to them, "Render to Caesar the things that are Caesar's, and to God the things that are God's." And they marveled at him."

Mark 12:13-17 ESV

Jesus silenced the Pharisees and Herodians by His profound teaching. Underlying the instruction to give to Caesar what was Caesar's and to God what was God's was the encouragement to give yourself over to Him. You are an image bearer after all and are made in His likeness. Property and money issues pale in comparison to this act of the will.

"And he sat down opposite the treasury and watched the people putting money into the offering box. Many rich people put in large sums. And a poor widow came and put in two small copper coins, which make a penny. And he called his disciples to him and said to them, "Truly, I say to you, this poor widow has put in more than all those who are contributing to the offering box. For they all contributed out of their abundance, but she out of her poverty has put in everything she had, all she had to live on."

Mark 12:41-44 ESV

This example and the importance given to it by Jesus communicates His heart so clearly. We are called to give. We are not called to give under certain circumstances or as a last priority in our growing list of responsibilities. We are called to give what we have, even if the amount adds up to a fraction of a single penny today (each coin was worth approximately 1/128th of a day's wages). Worth and value and sacrifice hold weight in the kingdom of God. Let's learn this truth and stop holding ourselves to a standard that says money is the key to pleasing God's heart.

Additional Reading: Matthew 22:15-22, Luke 20:19-26, Luke 21:1-4

▶ Write about a time you have practically given to God what is God's. What feelings did you experience at the time?

▶ In what ways did the story of the widow giving all she had stir up a desire to give inside of you? In what ways are you giving from what you have and not your abundance today?

▶ What was the most convicting aspect of these two passages of Scripture for you? Pay attention to the lessons and understand the priority Jesus placed on them given that He addressed them in culture in His final days.

DOER OF THE WORD

How can you apply what you have heard today? (James 1:22)

SABBATH: REST AND RENEW

PRAISE GOD. REPENT OF SIN. ASK FOR OTHERS + YOURSELF.
YIELD TO GOD. WAIT AND LISTEN.

Welcome to Sabbath. Today is a day of rest, reflection and restoration. I encourage you to find some quiet in your day today, get alone, pray and recharge. We practice this as followers of Jesus, emulating His ways and getting alone to rest.

After [Jesus] had dismissed [the crowds], he went up on a mountainside by himself to pray. When evening came, he was [still] there alone."

Matthew 14:23 ESV

Very early in the morning, while it was still dark, Jesus got up, left the house and went off to a solitary place, where he prayed.

Mark 1:35 ESV

Refer back to the first week's entry on Sabbath to remind yourself of the things you identified as most restful to you as well as what is helpful for you when trying to hear from God. Choose today how you'll implement one or more of these suggestions. Pay attention here to how God wired you to respond to Him. It may be unique to how others experience Him. It may be very similar. The goal is not to have a relationship with Jesus like someone else does. Learn to see your unique makeup as what leads you into deeper relationship and connection. Explore that today.

Below are some questions to ponder and respond to in order to help process what the Lord has been doing in your heart. Don't worry about looking up what you've written down in prior days and repeating those answers here. Really seek the Lord and ask Him the following:

▶ *What is one truth that has stayed with me from last week?*

▶ *How would you have me apply that one truth or one lesson for this coming week?*

▶ *What do you think of me? What do you think of my heart?*

Come back and journal here about your day before you go to sleep.

▶ *What did you learn about God on your Sabbath?*

▶ *What did you learn about yourself?*

▶ *What do you need to do or not do next time to make for a more holy Sabbath?*

▶ *Anything else you learned or realized or noticed today?*

DOER OF THE WORD

How can you apply what you have heard today? (James 1:22)

POURED OUT AND HAIR DOWN

PRAISE GOD. REPENT OF SIN. ASK FOR OTHERS + YOURSELF.
YIELD TO GOD. WAIT AND LISTEN.

"Six days before the Passover, Jesus therefore came to Bethany, where Lazarus was, whom Jesus had raise d from the dead. So they gave a dinner for him there. Martha served, and Lazarus was one of those reclining with him at table. Mary therefore took a pound of expensive ointment made from pure nard, and anointed the feet of Jesus and wiped his feet with her hair. The house was filled with the fragrance of the perfume. But Judas Iscariot, one of his disciples (he who was about to betray him), said, "Why was this ointment not sold for three hundred denarii and given to the poor?" He said this, not because he cared about the poor, but because he was a thief, and having charge of the moneybag he used to help himself to what was put into it. Jesus said, "Leave her alone, so that she may keep it for the day of my burial. For the poor you always have with you, but you do not always have me."

John 12:1-8 ESV

Jesus characterized this act of worship and devotion to Him as "a beautiful thing". He also stated wherever the gospel is proclaimed that Mary's actions would be told in memory of her. One unpopular decision to everyone around her at the time, except for Jesus, that demonstrated her pure heart of love for her Savior has us talking and thinking thousands of year later.

Additional Reading: Matthew 26:6-13, Mark 14:3-9

▶ Write about a time you made an unpopular decision with those around you in deference to your relationship with God. What were your thoughts and feelings when you thought about it later that day?

▶ Do you give to Jesus as freely as you give to causes you believe in? Why or why not?

▶ Mary had seen Jesus' devotion to her and those closest to them. Anointing His feet with her hair was remarkable in demonstrating her intense devotion to Him. She was humble in her outward actions. What have you learned most today in observing her demeanor and dedication to Jesus as Lord?

> DOER OF THE WORD <

How can you apply what you have heard today? (James 1:22)

PRAYER: ENGAGE AND ENJOY

PRAISE GOD. REPENT OF SIN. ASK FOR OTHERS + YOURSELF.
YIELD TO GOD. WAIT AND LISTEN.

Today will be all about prayer. Prayer can take on many forms, but at its heart it is connecting with the heart of God through praising, asking, repenting and responding to His will for your life. It can be done while on your knees in a worshipful posture with your head down, while walking/running down the street, through singing with arms raised or through quiet solitude alone. So challenge yourself during these days to pray in different ways to explore the depths of your relationship with the Lord.

If the questions below are helpful for you, please use them as a guide during this time today. If you feel strongly led to engage with God in a different way that's more meaningful or personal this week, please use this time for that. While the questions and ways of praying will be the same each week, I can guarantee the actual words used, words received from God, thoughts and experiences of forgiveness, love, confusion, pain, etc. will be very different from week to week. Use the truths that you've learned in your study time and lean on the Scripture and promises that have been discovered.

Engage your heart. Enjoy the process and connection with your Creator.

- *Jesus, I want to glorify and praise you today for...*

- *This week I've felt compelled to go deeper in this area:_____*
- ▶ *I pray today that you would speak to me concerning my area of deepest need. What would you have to say to me today?*

- Lord, this week I want to confess to you where I've been most convicted. Write below where you feel God challenging you the most. This will be hard but fight for your heart in this process and be honest about where He is gently but firmly bringing His purposes to light in your life. Repent from sin. Embrace freedom in Christ.

- Jesus teaches us to long for heaven. His life was a piece of heaven coming down to Earth for us. Ask Him for His will to be done on Earth as it is in heaven. Pray for His kingdom to come to Earth and write your prayer and/ or response below.

DOER OF THE WORD

How can you apply what you have heard today? (James 1:22)

SEVEN WOES

PRAISE GOD. REPENT OF SIN. ASK FOR OTHERS + YOURSELF.
YIELD TO GOD. WAIT AND LISTEN.

"Then Jesus said to the crowds and to his disciples, "The scribes and the Pharisees sit on Moses' seat, so do and observe whatever they tell you, but not the works they do. For they preach, but do not practice. They tie up heavy burdens, hard to bear, and lay them on people's shoulders, but they themselves are not willing to move them with their finger. They do all their deeds to be seen by others. For they make their phylacteries broad and their fringes long, and they love the place of honor at feasts and the best seats in the synagogues and greetings in the marketplaces and being called rabbi by others. But you are not to be called rabbi, for you have one teacher, and you are all brothers. And call no man your father on earth, for you have one Father, who is in heaven. Neither be called instructors, for you have one instructor, the Christ. The greatest among you shall be your servant. Whoever exalts himself will be humbled, and whoever humbles himself will be exalted."

Matthew 23:1-12 ESV

"And the Lord said to him, "Now you Pharisees cleanse the outside of the cup and of the dish, but inside you are full of greed and wickedness."

Luke 11:39 ESV

Additional Reading: Mark 12:38-39, Luke 11:37-54, Matthew 23:1-36

▶ It's interesting that Jesus encourages His people to listen to the scribes and Pharisees but in the same breath tells them to not emulate their behavior. Can you learn from imperfect sources of information? What obstacles do you need to get through for this to happen?

• Read the entirety of Matthew 23:1-36. Below identify two woes that you recognize as destructive towards a believer and non-believer alike. Write about a time where you've seen this behavior and how Jesus has taught to counteract this behavior in the Sermon on the Mount (Matthew 5, 6, 7).

Woe 1:_____

Counteractive Teaching:_____

Woe 2:_____

Counteractive Teaching:_____

DOER OF THE WORD

How can you apply what you have heard today? (James 1:22)

WEEK FOUR

LIGHT BRINGS FREEDOM

PRAISE GOD. REPENT OF SIN. ASK FOR OTHERS + YOURSELF.
YIELD TO GOD. WAIT AND LISTEN.

Freedom enables you to live towards something. No matter the obstacles or hardships that will occur, the idea of freedom exerts its influence over the things that can so easily entangle you. Darkness if you will.

• *Read John 1:1-18 and write out verse 5.*

Being a Dad has truly given me a different perspective on freedom. I have watched as tiny day old babies that I swaddled at night and rocked to sleep night after night have transitioned into discovering their own voice and letting their feelings be known to whoever will listen.

They feel absolute freedom probably 99.9% of the time to share their feelings and emotions with me, regardless if I want them or not.

My girls are hard wired to push against boundaries. It's something that is a part of our DNA. If you allow us to play a game with you or want to sit down to have a conversation or even take us on a shopping trip, inevitably we will find the boundaries of our circumstances and adjust from there.

I always enjoyed this aspect of my personality. In fact, it's what attracted me most to my bride. Yet as I continuously was invited into a fight with my girls nearly every time I challenged their desires to be masters of their own domain, I slowly started losing my appreciation for the work Jesus had done in my own heart and the context of our lives.

▶ *What does John 1:12 says can happen for us?*

BLOW OUT ONE CANDLE
(YOU SHOULD HAVE 4 LIT)

This verse says we can be children of God. If we receive Jesus, if we believe in His name, this verse says we have the right to become children of God. Such grace. It wasn't until I had kids that I allowed myself to see myself as a child of God. I saw my constant asking, my free dump of words to Him about whatever I wanted to talk about and realized I didn't fear a response from Him. I just felt safe.

Isn't that true freedom? When you believe so deeply in those that you trust, only then can you be unapologetically yourself. You can live with all the flaws, all the scars, all the open wounds and all the insecurities and still show your full self to the One who holds your future so firmly in His hands.

He loves you just as a Dad would love His children. He sees you. His words will both challenge and correct your default positions about life and how it should be lived. Jesus introduces you to a full and abundant life (John 10:10). Within the lessons of His life, the way He sacrificed and wept with and fought for His people, He has willingly experienced the darkness of our world and offered complete and total healing from the destruction of it.

▶ *Have you "received Him?" Do you "believe in His name?" Share how this happened for you.*

• *Read again John 1:18 and also John 14:6-7 and identify how God chose to reveal Himself to you.*

Knowing God has been the key reason so many real lives have been changed. History is full of stories of men having uncommon influence due to an extraordinary freedom afforded to them by knowing Christ. When the world chooses to value effort and drive and power, believers of Christ look to His servant leadership as not just a life meant to inspire but something to emulate.

There is something to be said for the man who knows His security is not in a paycheck or in a career. His identity is not found in the praises of others or torn down by the depths of failure. His influence doesn't rise and fall by the amount of time or money he's willing to spend with powerful people. Finding freedom in Christ enables life to be lived upstream of culture. It focuses the heart on experiencing surrender of self and submission to His will. It begs us to take up a posture of humility and lean fully into the freedom that is only offered in Christ.

"For freedom Christ has set us free; stand firm therefore, and do not submit again to a yoke of slavery."

Galatians 5:1 ESV

DOER OF THE WORD

How can you apply what you have heard today? (James 1:22)

JUSTICE: SINNERS

PRAISE GOD. REPENT OF SIN. ASK FOR OTHERS + YOURSELF.
YIELD TO GOD. WAIT AND LISTEN.

- *Write out Micah 6:8 and then circle the three things we should do.*

The Message translates this passage, *"But he's already made it plain how to live, what to do, what God is looking for in men and women. It's quite simple: Do what is fair and just to your neighbor, be compassionate and loyal in your love, And don't take yourself too seriously— take God seriously."*

First, let's look at this topic internally. Where do you, <insert name here>, identify with sinners? Justice is not about serving only. It's absolutely not about an "us vs. them" mentality. If these types of barriers exist in any way today or if we have a desire to serve simply out of duty or obligation, I want to connect with God's heart and see if He can't bring healing to our brokenness.

- *Romans 3:23 says "for all have sinned and fall short of the glory of God". In what ways do you identify as a sinner today? List out 2 or 3 things that come to mind.*

Jesus, we know who we are without You. I pray that we would not achieve our way out of our sin or believe the lie that we can outrun it. We need You to work in the midst of our chaos and redeem what has been fractured for our whole lives. Jesus, let your life be sanctifying for us. Forgive us of our sins. They're constant, they're consistent and they're hurtful. I ask that you would heal the wounds that have been projected onto me from other sinners. We ask for your wholeness in the messiness of life. I pray You would let us experience your grace today. Let me forgive those who have wronged me and be released from the effect it had on me. Bring light to our dark world and let us experience hope when we see your influence over sin in our own lives and the lives of others. We pray these things in Jesus' name. Amen.

Next, let's take this heart to those around us.

▶ *Who are sinners that have directly impacted you? Write their names or initials below.*

Maybe it's just me, but I find that compassion for myself and those that I don't know seems to be a lot higher than those that I know personally. As a consequence of knowing them, I've now given them something us sinners have been tripping over for generations. Expectations.

▶ *What are some expectations that have been placed on someone that has let you down?*

How can you speak healing into those people today? Maybe through an apology or maybe with a hug. Realizing that there isn't always ill intent and there isn't always perfect behavior goes a long way. I was told once that if you allowed a person three mistakes you'd likely gain a friend instead of an enemy. Maybe just seeing yourself and others a little deeper than normal will help give you a heart of compassion. Brokenness and pain have a way of showing up again and again and it usually affects those closest to us.

For someone you don't know, are there any opportunities today to impact their life for the better? If you've experienced the grace of Jesus, who can you share that experience with as a way to bring hope to someone who is wallowing in self pity or regret or despair? There is no condemnation in Jesus. His sacrifice on the cross atoned for all of our sin. All of our shortcomings. All of their shortcomings. There is no other reconciliation or activity that we can take part in that will take away the sin like He can.

Last, I'd like to address a ministry that is very close to our hearts. Those who are in prison today are simply sinners like you and me who are serving in a very public way. Often it's humbling, extremely uncomfortable, and lonely. Could you reach out to an inmate today? Could you give a day of your time to talk to them, get to know their stories and their names and offer your friendship? Sinners are people. We all know them. We are them.

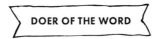

> DOER OF THE WORD

In light of what you've written, read and thought about, what is one thing you can do today to take care of sinners? (James 1:22)

THE GREATEST AND NEWEST COMMANDMENT

PRAISE GOD. REPENT OF SIN. ASK FOR OTHERS + YOURSELF.
YIELD TO GOD. WAIT AND LISTEN.

A new commandment I give to you, that you love one another: just as I have loved you, you also are to love one another. By this all people will know that you are my disciples, if you have love for one another.""

John 13:34-35 ESV

"But when the Pharisees heard that he had silenced the Sadducees, they gathered together. And one of them, a lawyer, asked him a question to test him. "Teacher, which is the great commandment in the Law?" And he said to him, "You shall love the Lord your God with all your heart and with all your soul and with all your mind. This is the great and first commandment. And a second is like it: You shall love your neighbor as yourself. On these two commandments depend all the Law and the Prophets.""

Matthew 22:34-40 ESV

Additional Reading: Mark 12:28-34, Romans 13:8-10, 1 John 4:10-12

▶ Why would Jesus draw attention in His final days to these two commandments specifically?

▶ Which comes easier to you - loving God or loving others? What things keep you from loving both God and others. These can be the same thing(s) or different, but ask God to remove these barriers once you recognize them as a hindrance to your faith.

▶ In Mark's account, Jesus says the lawyer is not far from the Kingdom of God. What continues to stand in the way of him experiencing Jesus as Savior if his thoughts and beliefs on the commandments are right?

DOER OF THE WORD

How can you apply what you have heard today? (James 1:22)

SABBATH: REST AND RENEW

PRAISE GOD. REPENT OF SIN. ASK FOR OTHERS + YOURSELF. YIELD TO GOD. WAIT AND LISTEN.

Welcome to Sabbath. Today is a day of rest, reflection and restoration. I encourage you to find some quiet in your day today, get alone, pray and recharge. We practice this as followers of Jesus, emulating His ways and getting alone to rest.

After [Jesus] had dismissed [the crowds], he went up on a mountainside by himself to pray. When evening came, he was [still] there alone."

Matthew 14:23 ESV

Very early in the morning, while it was still dark, Jesus got up, left the house and went off to a solitary place, where he prayed.

Mark 1:35 ESV

Refer back to the first week's entry on Sabbath to remind yourself of the things you identified as most restful to you as well as what is helpful for you when trying to hear from God. Choose today how you'll implement one or more of these suggestions. Pay attention here to how God wired you to respond to Him. It may be unique to how others experience Him. It may be very similar. The goal is not to have a relationship with Jesus like someone else does. Learn to see your unique makeup as what leads you into deeper relationship and connection. Explore that today.

Below are some questions to ponder and respond to in order to help process what the Lord has been doing in your heart. Don't worry about looking up what you've written down in prior days and repeating those answers here. Really seek the Lord and ask Him the following:

▶ *What is one truth that has stayed with me from last week?*

▶ *How would you have me apply that one truth or one lesson for this coming week?*

▶ *What do you think of me? What do you think of my heart?*

Come back and journal here about your day before you go to sleep.

▶ *What did you learn about God on your Sabbath?*

▶ *What did you learn about yourself?*

▶ *What do you need to do or not do next time to make for a more holy Sabbath?*

▶ *Anything else you learned or realized or noticed today?*

DOER OF THE WORD

How can you apply what you have heard today? (James 1:22)

TALENTS AND ENOUGH-NESS

PRAISE GOD. REPENT OF SIN. ASK FOR OTHERS + YOURSELF.
YIELD TO GOD. WAIT AND LISTEN.

"For it will be like a man going on a journey, who called his servants and entrusted to them his property. To one he gave five talents, to another two, to another one, to each according to his ability. Then he went away. He who had received the five talents went at once and traded with them, and he made five talents more. So also he who had the two talents made two talents more. But he who had received the one talent went and dug in the ground and hid his master's money. Now after a long time the master of those servants came and settled accounts with them. And he who had received the five talents came forward, bringing five talents more, saying, 'Master, you delivered to me five talents; here I have made five talents more.' His master said to him, 'Well done, good and faithful servant. You have been faithful over a little; I will set you over much. Enter into the joy of your master.' And he also who had the two talents came forward, saying, 'Master, you delivered to me two talents; here I have made two talents more.' His master said to him, 'Well done, good and faithful servant. You have been faithful over a little; I will set you over much. Enter into the joy of your master.' He also who had received the one talent came forward, saying, 'Master, I knew you to be a hard man, reaping where you did not sow, and gathering where you scattered no seed, so I was afraid, and I went and hid your talent in the ground. Here you have what is yours.' But his master answered him, 'You wicked and slothful servant! You knew that I reap where I have not sown and gather where I scattered no seed? Then you ought to have invested my money with the bankers, and at my coming I should have received what was my own with interest. So take the talent from him and give it to him who has the ten talents. For to everyone who has will more be given, and he will have an abundance. But from the one who has not, even what he has will be taken away. And cast the worthless servant into the outer darkness. In that place there will be weeping and gnashing of teeth.'"

Matthew 25:14-30 ESV

It's important to note the principal behind this teaching. One talent was worth roughly $600k in US currency. Bottom line is that all were given an amount of money that they could do something with. The principal of using your gifts and producing something as a result is key to following Jesus. It's an aspect of faith that should not be discounted and gives us a glimpse of what the kingdom of heaven will be like.

Additional Reading: Luke 19:12-27

▶ What stands out about Jesus' teaching about the talents and results of using your gifts productively?

• The most interesting aspect of this passage is the statement that faithfulness in this area allows you to "enter into the joy of your master"? Write what you think this will be like and find any Scriptures to support your thoughts and feelings.

▶ Here Jesus is not just encouraging you to have faith but is putting some real life application around the practice of faith and the use of your unique gifts. Have you embraced this idea that you should explore your strengths and see the opportunity to invest and reap the fruits of investment as something tied to your faith and belief in God instead of an idea that is solely about personal advancement? Why or why not?

⟩ DOER OF THE WORD ⟨

How can you apply what you have heard today? (James 1:22)

PRAYER: ENGAGE AND ENJOY

PRAISE GOD. REPENT OF SIN. ASK FOR OTHERS + YOURSELF.
YIELD TO GOD. WAIT AND LISTEN.

Today will be all about prayer. Prayer can take on many forms, but at its heart it is connecting with the heart of God through praising, asking, repenting and responding to His will for your life. It can be done while on your knees in a worshipful posture with your head down, while walking/running down the street, through singing with arms raised or through quiet solitude alone. So challenge yourself during these days to pray in different ways to explore the depths of your relationship with the Lord.

If the questions below are helpful for you, please use them as a guide during this time today. If you feel strongly led to engage with God in a different way that's more meaningful or personal this week, please use this time for that. While the questions and ways of praying will be the same each week, I can guarantee the actual words used, words received from God, thoughts and experiences of forgiveness, love, confusion, pain, etc. will be very different from week to week. Use the truths that you've learned in your study time and lean on the Scripture and promises that have been discovered.

Engage your heart. Enjoy the process and connection with your Creator.

- *Jesus, I want to glorify and praise you today for...*

- *This week I've felt compelled to go deeper in this area:_____*
- ▶ *I pray today that you would speak to me concerning my area of deepest need. What would you have to say to me today?*

- Lord, this week I want to confess to you where I've been most convicted. Write below where you feel God challenging you the most. This will be hard but fight for your heart in this process and be honest about where He is gently but firmly bringing His purposes to light in your life. Repent from sin. Embrace freedom in Christ.

- Jesus teaches us to long for heaven. His life was a piece of heaven coming down to Earth for us. Ask Him for His will to be done on Earth as it is in heaven. Pray for His kingdom to come to Earth and write your prayer and/or response below.

> DOER OF THE WORD <

How can you apply what you have heard today? (James 1:22)

DIRTY FEET CLEAN

PRAISE GOD. REPENT OF SIN. ASK FOR OTHERS + YOURSELF.
YIELD TO GOD. WAIT AND LISTEN.

"Now before the Feast of the Passover, when Jesus knew that his hour had come to depart out of this world to the Father, having loved his own who were in the world, he loved them to the end. During supper, when the devil had already put it into the heart of Judas Iscariot, Simon's son, to betray him, Jesus, knowing that the Father had given all things into his hands, and that he had come from God and was going back to God, rose from supper.

He laid aside his outer garments, and taking a towel, tied it around his waist. Then he poured water into a basin and began to wash the disciples' feet and to wipe them with the towel that was wrapped around him. He came to Simon Peter, who said to him, "Lord, do you wash my feet?" Jesus answered him, "What I am doing you do not understand now, but afterward you will understand." Peter said to him, "You shall never wash my feet." Jesus answered him, "If I do not wash you, you have no share with me." Simon Peter said to him, "Lord, not my feet only but also my hands and my head!" Jesus said to him, "The one who has bathed does not need to wash, except for his feet, but is completely clean. And you are clean, but not every one of you."

For he knew who was to betray him; that was why he said, "Not all of you are clean." When he had washed their feet and put on his outer garments and resumed his place, he said to them, "Do you understand what I have done to you? You call me Teacher and Lord, and you are right, for so I am. If I then, your Lord and Teacher, have washed your feet, you also ought to wash one another's feet. For I have given you an example, that you also should do just as I have done to you.

Truly, truly, I say to you, a servant is not greater than his master, nor is a messenger greater than the one who sent him. If you know these things, blessed are you if you do them. I am not speaking of all of you; I know whom I have chosen. But the Scripture will be fulfilled, 'He who ate my bread has lifted his heel against me.' I am telling you this now, before it takes place, that when it does take place you may believe that I am he. Truly, truly, I say to you, whoever receives the one I send receives me, and whoever receives me receives the one who sent me."

John 13:1-20 ESV

▶ Why is Jesus washing the disciples' feet? What is He demonstrating for them to follow once He's gone? Hint: write about the principal of His teaching, not just the washing of the feet.

▶ Similar to Peter, where in your life have you refused Jesus' service towards you?

▶ How does this passage challenge your worldview about leadership and service?

> DOER OF THE WORD <

How can you apply what you have heard today? (James 1:22)

WEEK FIVE

HIS WORD BRINGS LIGHT

PRAISE GOD. REPENT OF SIN. ASK FOR OTHERS + YOURSELF.
YIELD TO GOD. WAIT AND LISTEN.

Light is the ultimate enabler. Back when the US was founded, we had two diplomats in France tasked with gaining French support for American Independence. One was John Adams, our 2nd president. The other was Benjamin Franklin, one of our most famous founding fathers.

What may not be as well known was the dislike they had for each other while on this particular assignment. John Adams was the epitome of a statesman. Early to bed, early to rise. Respectful in all manners of speech and action. He seemed to grasp how fragile this venture would be and thus took calculated steps to make sure all interaction was handled appropriately and purposefully. He would frequently start his days at 4 AM, light a candle and write his letters back home.

In one or more of these letters, Mr. Adams described Mr. Franklin in unflattering terms. He labeled him as someone who enjoyed strong drink, who would never dare to miss a party or reason to gather with others and who criticized his sleeping and waking habits at length. He could not for the life of him understand what good could come from someone staying up past 7:30 or 8 pm. Keep in mind this was before electricity, so in order to stay up candles had to be present and even then there had to be enough to light a room (which would be quite the undertaking!).

Benjamin Franklin would stay out until 9 pm and sleep in all the way until about 7 or 7:30 am. Think what you will about his habits or even his shortcomings, but Benjamin Franklin possessed a knowledge that many of us need to learn. He knew that the presence of light could enable so much more than the presence of darkness.

- *Read Psalm 119:97-105. Write down the main idea of this passage of Scripture.*

▶ *Evaluate where you are in life. Do you desire His word? Do you have time for it?*

BLOW OUT ONE CANDLE

(YOU SHOULD HAVE 3 LIT)

▶ *Does it offer all that the psalmist writes about? If not, do you believe it could?*

I share this story because I love the illustration. If light enables aspects of life that would not be possible without it, then we must ask the question what gives us light? The ritual we're repeating again this week is slowly blowing out candles to signify the darkness we would find ourselves in without Jesus.

This passage of Scripture speaks to our desire for His word and what our reaction should be when we're able to read it. The psalmist has spent time in it, has sat with it, has pondered it, has remembered its laws, and has found meaning in gaining wisdom. He goes so far to say that God's word is a "lamp to my feet and a light to my path."

Our exercise today is aimed at waking the desire within you to read, understand and apply God's word in your life. First step is to pick a verse that you a particularly drawn to for one reason or another. I don't want to offer examples as I want this to be something that comes from you. Search on your Bible app, use a concordance or choose one by memory, but pick a verse that speaks to you.

• *Write down your verse.*

Next, commit to writing the verse down every morning until next Sunday. Don't try to memorize it, but do try to write it down once. See the main idea of the verse and read the verses around it so you are learning the meaning within context.

Last, repeat the main idea to yourself when appropriate during the day. If your verse is on anger, repeat it to yourself after you get angry (or even better as you feel it rising within you). As you write it throughout the week or when you go to repeat it to yourself, you will likely start remembering the actual words in Scripture and committing it to memory. If that happens great. If not, make sure you're keeping with you the meaning behind the verse.

There's no magic in God's word that will change your circumstances or thought patterns instantaneously. I suppose it could happen, but I tend to think of Scripture like a relationship. The more you spend time with it, the more you lean into your confusion, the more you ask of it and the more willing your heart is to grow when interacting with it, the more effective it will be.

Don't let these words remain in a book that stays on your shelf for decoration. These words offer life and bring Jesus' light to your everyday. Let these words be life giving to you.

DOER OF THE WORD

How can you apply what you have heard today? (James 1:22)

JUSTICE: THE HUNGRY

PRAISE GOD. REPENT OF SIN. ASK FOR OTHERS + YOURSELF.
YIELD TO GOD. WAIT AND LISTEN.

- *Write out Micah 6:8 and then circle the three things we should do.*

The Message translates this passage, *"But he's already made it plain how to live, what to do, what God is looking for in men and women. It's quite simple: Do what is fair and just to your neighbor, be compassionate and loyal in your love, And don't take yourself too seriously— take God seriously."*

First, let's look at this topic internally. Where do you, <insert name here>, identify with the hungry? Justice is not about serving only. It's absolutely not about an "us vs. them" mentality. If these types of barriers exist in any way today or if we have a desire to serve simply out of duty or obligation, I want to connect with God's heart and see if He can't bring healing to our brokenness.

▶ *In what ways are you hungry today? List out 2 or 3 things that come to mind.*

Jesus, hunger can mean so many things in our world. For those of us that have regular meals, I pray that the hunger we feel before meals will help us realize that our reality is not everyone's and that there is suffering happening all around us. Even if it's in small ways, we do know what hunger feels like. Thank you for this feeling. Let us see You clearly as Provider and Lord when we eat as you meet our needs. I thank you for food that sustains us, that stirs memories of past meals and those we were able to share those meals with. I pray that hunger we experience while fasting would be purposeful. I pray our dependence on You would be real and that we wouldn't fall into the trap of thinking we can provide for our needs whenever we have them. Spiritually, let us hunger and thirst for righteousness. It would drive so many of our priorities and follow through, just like food does. May hunger be a real teacher to us today and in future days. We pray these things in Jesus' name. Amen.

Next, let's take this heart to those around us.

▶ *Who are people you know that are hungry? Write their names or initials below.*

Depending on where you're reading this study from, our experiences with hunger can be very different. Instead of getting into specifics, in hope that all of us can find an outlet to rally around that applies to our reality, I want to talk about a few groups who experience hunger and have a real need that you can meet.

One is the homeless. Regardless of circumstance, there are many in your city or one close by that do not have a regular place to sleep at night or call home. They don't have refrigerators or freezers or money to grab fast food or a nice meal out whenever they feel like it. A couple of ways you could help out would be to volunteer at a homeless shelter by serving food or eating a meal with those that are there. You could hand out a snack bag with an apple, granola bar and a bottle of water while you're waiting at a stop light. You could donate to a ministry overseas who directly works with those without food and meet a need that way.

Next are those that are hungry for varying circumstances. When I was in college, I was 20 hours away from home and didn't get back very often. Thanksgiving meals or a dinner with a family from church are still moments I cherish deeply today. I learned more about life during those times than in the classroom when someone decided to save a seat for me at their table. Open up your home and invite a student over.

Last, your neighbors. Communities and relationships are often strengthened and built over the dinner table. When you live in community, you often find out about needs of those directly around you that you wouldn't have otherwise known about. Invite your neighbors over for dinner to get to know them. Set up a lemonade stand with your kids in your driveway. If someone close to you has more on their schedule than normal, has experienced the loss of a family member or is low on funds for a month, meet the need in a way that only you can meet it. You may be the only person that knows about their hunger.

DOER OF THE WORD

In light of what you've written, read and thought about, what is one thing you can do today to take care of the hungry? (James 1:22)

THE BEST BREAD AND WINE EVER

PRAISE GOD. REPENT OF SIN. ASK FOR OTHERS + YOURSELF.
YIELD TO GOD. WAIT AND LISTEN.

"Then came the day of Unleavened Bread, on which the Passover lamb had to be sacrificed. So Jesus sent Peter and John, saying, "Go and prepare the Passover for us, that we may eat it." They said to him, "Where will you have us prepare it?" He said to them, "Behold, when you have entered the city, a man carrying a jar of water will meet you. Follow him into the house that he enters and tell the master of the house, 'The Teacher says to you, Where is the guest room, where I may eat the Passover with my disciples?' And he will show you a large upper room furnished; prepare it there." And they went and found it just as he had told them, and they prepared the Passover.

And when the hour came, he reclined at table, and the apostles with him. And he said to them, "I have earnestly desired to eat this Passover with you before I suffer. For I tell you I will not eat it until it is fulfilled in the kingdom of God." And he took a cup, and when he had given thanks he said, "Take this, and divide it among yourselves. For I tell you that from now on I will not drink of the fruit of the vine until the kingdom of God comes."

And he took bread, and when he had given thanks, he broke it and gave it to them, saying, "This is my body, which is given for you. Do this in remembrance of me." And likewise the cup after they had eaten, saying, "This cup that is poured out for you is the new covenant in my blood. But behold, the hand of him who betrays me is with me on the table. For the Son of Man goes as it has been determined, but woe to that man by whom he is betrayed!" And they began to question one another, which of them it could be who was going to do this."

Luke 22:7-23 ESV

Jesus here, through the symbolism of the wine as His blood, is sealing a new covenant and stating that from now on, those who believe in Him and take the bread and wine in remembrance of Him will be protected from ultimate judgment due to Jesus' blood being shed for them. His final Passover meal was spent revealing His true nature and purpose to His disciples.

Additional Reading: Matthew 26:17-25; Matthew 26:26-29, Mark 14:12-25

▶ Can you imagine the sorrow of the disciples? Put yourself in their shoes. What feelings would you experience hearing the news that one of your closest brothers was going to betray your Lord and Savior?

▶ In Luke 22:15, it says that Jesus "earnestly desired to eat this Passover with you before I suffer". Why did He look forward to it so much?

▶ Jesus must've felt the weight of this moment. I picture it as being hope fulfilled mixed with the depth of despair due to the betrayal and impending suffering. What effect did fear have on Jesus' final days, if any? What did it drive Him to do?

DOER OF THE WORD

How can you apply what you have heard today? (James 1:22)

SABBATH: REST AND RENEW

PRAISE GOD. REPENT OF SIN. ASK FOR OTHERS + YOURSELF.
YIELD TO GOD. WAIT AND LISTEN.

Welcome to Sabbath. Today is a day of rest, reflection and restoration. I encourage you to find some quiet in your day today, get alone, pray and recharge. We practice this as followers of Jesus, emulating His ways and getting alone to rest.

After [Jesus] had dismissed [the crowds], he went up on a mountainside by himself to pray. When evening came, he was [still] there alone."

Matthew 14:23 ESV

Very early in the morning, while it was still dark, Jesus got up, left the house and went off to a solitary place, where he prayed.

Mark 1:35 ESV

Refer back to the first week's entry on Sabbath to remind yourself of the things you identified as most restful to you as well as what is helpful for you when trying to hear from God. Choose today how you'll implement one or more of these suggestions. Pay attention here to how God wired you to respond to Him. It may be unique to how others experience Him. It may be very similar. The goal is not to have a relationship with Jesus like someone else does. Learn to see your unique makeup as what leads you into deeper relationship and connection. Explore that today.

Below are some questions to ponder and respond to in order to help process what the Lord has been doing in your heart. Don't worry about looking up what you've written down in prior days and repeating those answers here. Really seek the Lord and ask Him the following:

▶ *What is one truth that has stayed with me from last week?*

▶ *How would you have me apply that one truth or one lesson for this coming week?*

▶ *What do you think of me? What do you think of my heart?*

Come back and journal here about your day before you go to sleep.

▶ *What did you learn about God on your Sabbath?*

▶ *What did you learn about yourself?*

▶ *What do you need to do or not do next time to make for a more holy Sabbath?*

▶ *Anything else you learned or realized or noticed today?*

DOER OF THE WORD

How can you apply what you have heard today? (James 1:22)

I DON'T KNOW HIM

PRAISE GOD. REPENT OF SIN. ASK FOR OTHERS + YOURSELF. YIELD TO GOD. WAIT AND LISTEN.

"And when they had sung a hymn, they went out to the Mount of Olives. And Jesus said to them, "You will all fall away, for it is written, 'I will strike the shepherd, and the sheep will be scattered.' But after I am raised up, I will go before you to Galilee." Peter said to him, "Even though they all fall away, I will not." And Jesus said to him, "Truly, I tell you, this very night, before the rooster crows twice, you will deny me three times." But he said emphatically, "If I must die with you, I will not deny you." And they all said the same."

Mark 14:26-31 ESV

Zechariah 13:7 is the verse that Jesus is referencing about the sheep being scattered. If you go on to read, in verse 9 it states that the Lord will place His sheep (i.e. Believers) into the fire to be refined as one refines silver. I like this illustration because of the nature of a silversmith. A silversmith knows when to take his metal out of the refining fire only when he can see his reflection in it. Powerful imagery for us as followers to understand our own refining times.

"And as Peter was below in the courtyard, one of the servant girls of the high priest came, and seeing Peter warming himself, she looked at him and said, "You also were with the Nazarene, Jesus." But he denied it, saying, "I neither know nor understand what you mean." And he went out into the gateway and the rooster crowed. And the servant girl saw him and began again to say to the bystanders, "This man is one of them." But again he denied it. And after a little while the bystanders again said to Peter, "Certainly you are one of them, for you are a Galilean." But he began to invoke a curse on himself and to swear, "I do not know this man of whom you speak." And immediately the rooster crowed a second time. And Peter remembered how Jesus had said to him, "Before the rooster crows twice, you will deny me three times." And he broke down and wept."

Mark 14:66-72 ESV

See Jesus' sovereignty over this period and His intimate knowledge of His followers and the fulfillment of prophecy.

Additional Reading: Matthew 26:30-35; Luke 22:31-34; John 13:36-38, Matthew 26:69-75; Luke 22:54-62; John 18:15-18

▶ Write about a time you have denied your relationship with God. What led to it and what resulted from it?

▶ Does relating the Lord's refinement of us to a silversmith refining metal help bring understanding to trials in your life? Have those trials made you reflect the likeness of your creator? How so?

▶ What is hardest for you to experience when living these final days with Jesus? How are you connecting with Him in new ways over these past few weeks?

> DOER OF THE WORD <

How can you apply what you have heard today? (James 1:22)

PRAYER: ENGAGE AND ENJOY

PRAISE GOD. REPENT OF SIN. ASK FOR OTHERS + YOURSELF.
YIELD TO GOD. WAIT AND LISTEN.

Today will be all about prayer. Prayer can take on many forms, but at its heart it is connecting with the heart of God through praising, asking, repenting and responding to His will for your life. It can be done while on your knees in a worshipful posture with your head down, while walking/running down the street, through singing with arms raised or through quiet solitude alone. So challenge yourself during these days to pray in different ways to explore the depths of your relationship with the Lord.

If the questions below are helpful for you, please use them as a guide during this time today. If you feel strongly led to engage with God in a different way that's more meaningful or personal this week, please use this time for that. While the questions and ways of praying will be the same each week, I can guarantee the actual words used, words received from God, thoughts and experiences of forgiveness, love, confusion, pain, etc. will be very different from week to week. Use the truths that you've learned in your study time and lean on the Scripture and promises that have been discovered.

Engage your heart. Enjoy the process and connection with your Creator.

• *Jesus, I want to glorify and praise you today for...*

• *This week I've felt compelled to go deeper in this area:_____*
▶ *I pray today that you would speak to me concerning my area of deepest need. What would you have to say to me today?*

- Lord, this week I want to confess to you where I've been most convicted. Write below where you feel God challenging you the most. This will be hard but fight for your heart in this process and be honest about where He is gently but firmly bringing His purposes to light in your life. Repent from sin. Embrace freedom in Christ.

- Jesus teaches us to long for heaven. His life was a piece of heaven coming down to Earth for us. Ask Him for His will to be done on Earth as it is in heaven. Pray for His kingdom to come to Earth and write your prayer and/or response below.

DOER OF THE WORD

How can you apply what you have heard today? (James 1:22)

QUESTIONS AND A HELPER

PRAISE GOD. REPENT OF SIN. ASK FOR OTHERS + YOURSELF.
YIELD TO GOD. WAIT AND LISTEN.

"Let not your hearts be troubled. Believe in God; believe also in me. In my Father's house are many rooms. If it were not so, would I have told you that I go to prepare a place for you? And if I go and prepare a place for you, I will come again and will take you to myself, that where I am you may be also. And you know the way to where I am going." Thomas said to him, "Lord, we do not know where you are going. How can we know the way?"

Jesus said to him, "I am the way, and the truth, and the life. No one comes to the Father except through me. If you had known me, you would have known my Father also. From now on you do know him and have seen him."

Philip said to him, "Lord, show us the Father, and it is enough for us." Jesus said to him, "Have I been with you so long, and you still do not know me, Philip? Whoever has seen me has seen the Father. How can you say, 'Show us the Father'? Do you not believe that I am in the Father and the Father is in me?

The words that I say to you I do not speak on my own authority, but the Father who dwells in me does his works. Believe me that I am in the Father and the Father is in me, or else believe on account of the works themselves. "Truly, truly, I say to you, whoever believes in me will also do the works that I do; and greater works than these will he do, because I am going to the Father. Whatever you ask in my name, this I will do, that the Father may be glorified in the Son. If you ask me anything in my name, I will do it."

John 14:1-14 ESV

▶ Jesus speaks directly to the disciples, preparing them for life after His death. Why do you think Jesus chooses to speak using direct words as opposed to a parable here?

▶ What is the source of all of Jesus' works on Earth? Does this explain His assuredness or the authority of His teaching?

• Finish this day with prayer asking God to do the greater works Jesus speaks about here in you. Surrender yourself and your life to the Lord by accepting Him as Lord and Savior. Choose to believe Jesus' words and His connection with the Father.

⟩ DOER OF THE WORD ⟨

How can you apply what you have heard today? (James 1:22)

WEEK SIX

HE LEADS THE BLIND

PRAISE GOD. REPENT OF SIN. ASK FOR OTHERS + YOURSELF.
YIELD TO GOD. WAIT AND LISTEN.

Well before Jesus was here on Earth, there was an abundance of prophecy about His life so that when He came He would be recognized, believed in and followed. We'll dig into one of those prophecies today which helps bring further clarity to the depth of meaning behind His final days.

• *Read Isaiah 42:16. Write out the verse.*

To understand more context around this verse, read Isaiah 42:1-7. I want to focus in on verse 6 and 7 specifically. The context of the chapter is God talking about His servant (Jesus) who will bring justice to the nations.

We often take blindness to mean physical blindness. We've explored this idea earlier in the study by thinking about all consuming darkness around us and recognizing which senses are our greatest strength. We even saw Jesus physically heal those who were blind during His ministry to both exert His influence over our reality and also assure our hearts that He sees and cares about our humanity and its shortcomings.

The Bible also addresses spiritual blindness, which is more what this passage is exploring. In verse 7 when God the Father speaks about opening the eyes of the blind and bringing prisoners out of the dungeon, He is using history as a teacher. The people of this time would have been familiar with the captivity of the Israelites in Babylon and thus would equate being set free from blindness to the people being set free from the Babylonian exile.

Think of how hopeful of a message this was to them. God wanted the people to recognize His servant who would fulfill all that the nation of Israel was designed to be. He would be their deliverer out of darkness and would lead the people who were spiritually blind. They could not lead themselves and this was God speaking directly to their fears, saying they would not be forsaken.

BLOW OUT ONE CANDLE

(YOU SHOULD HAVE 2 LIT)

▶ *Have you ever felt forsaken by God, even when His word says He will guide you in your spiritual blindness?*

• *Read Romans 8:24-28. Write out the main points of the passage in bullet form.*

Hope unseen should drive us to a place of desperation, of repentance and dependence. While we wait, this says, we wait with patience. In our spiritual blindness, as our faith is strong and even at times weak, these verses are encouraging reliance on the Spirit of God to bring words to our waiting prayers.

Ever feel like you're wandering in your prayers to God? You're not exactly sure how He's moving, yet you know the truth of Scripture that He has lived and died so that there may be redemption and salvation for you specifically. The Spirit groans on our behalf where words are simply inadequate (v. 26). This is "leading the blind" in practical terms.

Next time you're struggling to experience freedom in an area of your life, even if it only affects you in a small way, lean into the Spirit of God and ask that He intercedes on your behalf. Embrace the identity of a follower, a true believer. It's my hope that we can get out of this self-reliance mindset when it comes to our faith. It's destroying hearts of men that were created to live tethered to the will of God over their own. Yet detached from a guide or the word of God, we live as if our worth and purpose is wrapped up in only the things that we can see.

It's a trap. Jesus' days here with us taught us differently.

"And we know that for those who love God all things work together for good, for those who are called according to his purpose. For those whom he foreknew he also predestined to be conformed to the image of his Son..."

Romans 8:28-29a ESV

As much as verse 28 is shared in our culture, my hope for us is that we would champion verse 29 even more so. The good that is talked about here is not merely that your immediate needs would be met. Expand your capacity for satisfaction. This is saying the good actually means conformity to the image of Jesus. You will be made like Him.

Patiently trust His heart for the blind, for you, is moving you towards blind obedience to Him. May our trust and faith in Him be unshakeable today.

DOER OF THE WORD

How can you apply what you have heard today? (James 1:22)

JUSTICE: THE BROKEN-HEARTED

PRAISE GOD. REPENT OF SIN. ASK FOR OTHERS + YOURSELF. YIELD TO GOD. WAIT AND LISTEN.

- *Write out Micah 6:8 and then circle the three things we should do.*

The Message translates this passage, "But he's already made it plain how to live, what to do, what God is looking for in men and women. It's quite simple: Do what is fair and just to your neighbor, be compassionate and loyal in your love, And don't take yourself too seriously — take God seriously."

First, let's look at this topic internally. Where do you, <insert name here>, identify with the broken-hearted? Justice is not about serving only. It's absolutely not about an "us vs. them" mentality. If these types of barriers exist in any way today or if we have a desire to serve simply out of duty or obligation, I want to connect with God's heart and see if He can't bring healing to our brokenness.

▶ *In what ways are you broken-hearted today? List out 2 or 3 things that come to mind.*

Jesus, so much of what we experience through media or through interactions with people deal with broken hearts. We see a group of people who are treated horrifically by someone in power and our hearts break for their suffering. We see relationships end and kids grow up in broken homes and our hearts break for all that are involved. We ask that you be close to us in these days. I pray You would let us experience the pain of a broken heart only as long as is necessary to cement your will in our lives and move us to action. Protect our fragile hearts as they start to mend after an especially trying time. Show us people that are broken hearted today. Let us see them as we see ourselves, as people in need of a healing touch, a comforting word or a timely prayer. May your hope fill our hearts and the broken places that seem beyond repair. We pray these things in Jesus' name. Amen.

Next, let's take this heart to those around us.

▶ **Who are people you know that are broken-hearted? Write their names or initials below.**

"The Lord is near to the brokenhearted and saves the crushed in spirit."

Psalms 34:18 ESV

In speaking to someone who has a broken heart, the first thing we should be reminded of is that they're hurting. They're grieving. They're bleeding. They're desperately searching for hope. A broken hearted person is not looking for a critique of what brought them to their current state or advice on how to live their way out of it.

In these situations, broken hearts cry out for your full self to be present. The verse above is the only thing that has enabled me to do this. If I hug at the wrong time, if I say the wrong thing, if I offer advice while trying to be understanding... these questions often keep us from doing anything. We believe the lie that nothing would be better than something. The verse insures that if my worst fears do come to fruition and I do let the person I'm talking to down, then I have a God I can run to with my broken heart and one who will save me from my despair.

This is what we have to offer people. Not advice. Not strategy. Not justification. We have a treasure, whose name is Jesus, that cried with friends over the death of a brother. We have a Savior that ran to the diseased instead of away from them. Spending time with someone who is hurting can be so healing in the moment.

When we don't know what would be helpful to someone who is hurting and can't even get out the words because the pain is so deep, stay in the moment and wait. Pray over them in your head. Beg God to deliver them from their pain, even for a second. Don't discount their feelings or raw emotions in the time. Understand the brokenness that is being felt can have something to do with you or could have absolutely nothing to do with you. Yet do engage with that person. Be close to the broken-hearted, just as Jesus was. Reach out when you feel the pull. Love in the face of uncertainty.

DOER OF THE WORD

In light of what you've written, read and thought about, what is one thing you can do today to take care of the broken-hearted? (James 1:22)

IT'S OK TO BE HONEST

PRAISE GOD. REPENT OF SIN. ASK FOR OTHERS + YOURSELF.
YIELD TO GOD. WAIT AND LISTEN.

"Then Jesus went with them to a place called Gethsemane, and he said to his disciples, "Sit here, while I go over there and pray." And taking with him Peter and the two sons of Zebedee, he began to be sorrowful and troubled. Then he said to them, "My soul is very sorrowful, even to death; remain here, and watch with me."

And going a little farther he fell on his face and prayed, saying, "My Father, if it be possible, let this cup pass from me; nevertheless, not as I will, but as you will." And he came to the disciples and found them sleeping. And he said to Peter, "So, could you not watch with me one hour? Watch and pray that you may not enter into temptation. The spirit indeed is willing, but the flesh is weak."

Again, for the second time, he went away and prayed, "My Father, if this cannot pass unless I drink it, your will be done." And again he came and found them sleeping, for their eyes were heavy.

So, leaving them again, he went away and prayed for the third time, saying the same words again. Then he came to the disciples and said to them, "Sleep and take your rest later on. See, the hour is at hand, and the Son of Man is betrayed into the hands of sinners. Rise, let us be going; see, my betrayer is at hand.""

Matthew 26:36-46 ESV

Additional Reading: Mark 14:32-42; Luke 22:39-46

▶ Why did Jesus bring three of His disciples with Him to the garden? What does it say about the agony Jesus was in and the relationship He had with His closest followers?

▶ In Luke, it is recorded that Jesus asked His Father to remove the cup of suffering from Him. Even so, Hebrews 12:2 along with some other Scripture we will read in the coming days exalts the Lord for enduring the cross. What moved Him to follow through?

▶ This moment is often talked about, but it's made possible by Jesus' custom to get alone with the Father in this manner. His words, His emotions, His willingness to not be ok in this moment is a direct result from His relationship with the Father. How does this obedience and closeness challenge your current walk with the Lord?

DOER OF THE WORD

How can you apply what you have heard today? (James 1:22)

SABBATH: REST AND RENEW

PRAISE GOD. REPENT OF SIN. ASK FOR OTHERS + YOURSELF.
YIELD TO GOD. WAIT AND LISTEN.

Welcome to Sabbath. Today is a day of rest, reflection and restoration. I encourage you to find some quiet in your day today, get alone, pray and recharge. We practice this as followers of Jesus, emulating His ways and getting alone to rest.

After [Jesus] had dismissed [the crowds], he went up on a mountainside by himself to pray. When evening came, he was [still] there alone."

Matthew 14:23 ESV

Very early in the morning, while it was still dark, Jesus got up, left the house and went off to a solitary place, where he prayed.

Mark 1:35 ESV

Refer back to the first week's entry on Sabbath to remind yourself of the things you identified as most restful to you as well as what is helpful for you when trying to hear from God. Choose today how you'll implement one or more of these suggestions. Pay attention here to how God wired you to respond to Him. It may be unique to how others experience Him. It may be very similar. The goal is not to have a relationship with Jesus like someone else does. Learn to see your unique makeup as what leads you into deeper relationship and connection. Explore that today.

Below are some questions to ponder and respond to in order to help process what the Lord has been doing in your heart. Don't worry about looking up what you've written down in prior days and repeating those answers here. Really seek the Lord and ask Him the following:

▶ *What is one truth that has stayed with me from last week?*

▶ How would you have me apply that one truth or one lesson for this coming week?

▶ What do you think of me? What do you think of my heart?

Come back and journal here about your day before you go to sleep.

▶ What did you learn about God on your Sabbath?

▶ What did you learn about yourself?

▶ What do you need to do or not do next time to make for a more holy Sabbath?

▶ Anything else you learned or realized or noticed today?

DOER OF THE WORD

How can you apply what you have heard today? (James 1:22)

A KISS ON THE CHEEK

PRAISE GOD. REPENT OF SIN. ASK FOR OTHERS + YOURSELF.
YIELD TO GOD. WAIT AND LISTEN.

"While he was still speaking, there came a crowd, and the man called Judas, one of the twelve, was leading them. He drew near to Jesus to kiss him, but Jesus said to him, "Judas, would you betray the Son of Man with a kiss?" And when those who were around him saw what would follow, they said, "Lord, shall we strike with the sword?" And one of them struck the servant of the high priest and cut off his right ear. But Jesus said, "No more of this!" And he touched his ear and healed him. Then Jesus said to the chief priests and officers of the temple and elders, who had come out against him, "Have you come out as against a robber, with swords and clubs? When I was with you day after day in the temple, you did not lay hands on me. But this is your hour, and the power of darkness.""

Luke 22:47-53 ESV

"When Jesus had spoken these words, he went out with his disciples across the brook Kidron, where there was a garden, which he and his disciples entered. Now Judas, who betrayed him, also knew the place, for Jesus often met there with his disciples. So Judas, having procured a band of soldiers and some officers from the chief priests and the Pharisees, went there with lanterns and torches and weapons. Then Jesus, knowing all that would happen to him, came forward and said to them, "Whom do you seek?" They answered him, "Jesus of Nazareth." Jesus said to them, "I am he." Judas, who betrayed him, was standing with them. When Jesus said to them, "I am he," they drew back and fell to the ground. So he asked them again, "Whom do you seek?" And they said, "Jesus of Nazareth." Jesus answered, "I told you that I am he. So, if you seek me, let these men go." This was to fulfill the word that he had spoken: "Of those whom you gave me I have lost not one." Then Simon Peter, having a sword, drew it and struck the high priest's servant and cut off his right ear. (The servant's name was Malchus.) So Jesus said to Peter, "Put your sword into its sheath; shall I not drink the cup that the Father has given me?""

John 18:1-11 ESV

Additional Reading: Matthew 26:47-56; Mark 14:43-50

▶ Jesus heals one of the soldiers sent to capture Him immediately once Peter struck him on the ear. How does this deepen your faith in Jesus seeing His intention to preserve not just physical wholeness but spiritual wholeness of those that are against Him?

▶ In Mark's account of this story, he mentions the rituals of respect that Judas follows through with, such as calling Jesus "Rabbi" and kissing Him on the cheek. Why does he include that in His account?

▶ Jesus clearly is willing to step into His deity in this moment. This explains the soldiers dropping to the ground upon hearing His claim that "I am He." Have you ever approached your faith with this level of confidence? Have you ever found security in your identity as one of His own?

› DOER OF THE WORD ‹

How can you apply what you have heard today? (James 1:22)

PRAYER: ENGAGE AND ENJOY

PRAISE GOD. REPENT OF SIN. ASK FOR OTHERS + YOURSELF.
YIELD TO GOD. WAIT AND LISTEN.

Today will be all about prayer. Prayer can take on many forms, but at its heart it is connecting with the heart of God through praising, asking, repenting and responding to His will for your life. It can be done while on your knees in a worshipful posture with your head down, while walking/running down the street, through singing with arms raised or through quiet solitude alone. So challenge yourself during these days to pray in different ways to explore the depths of your relationship with the Lord.

If the questions below are helpful for you, please use them as a guide during this time today. If you feel strongly led to engage with God in a different way that's more meaningful or personal this week, please use this time for that. While the questions and ways of praying will be the same each week, I can guarantee the actual words used, words received from God, thoughts and experiences of forgiveness, love, confusion, pain, etc. will be very different from week to week. Use the truths that you've learned in your study time and lean on the Scripture and promises that have been discovered.

Engage your heart. Enjoy the process and connection with your Creator.

- *Jesus, I want to glorify and praise you today for...*

- *This week I've felt compelled to go deeper in this area:* _____
- ▶ *I pray today that you would speak to me concerning my area of deepest need. What would you have to say to me today?*

- Lord, this week I want to confess to you where I've been most convicted. Write below where you feel God challenging you the most. This will be hard but fight for your heart in this process and be honest about where He is gently but firmly bringing His purposes to light in your life. Repent from sin. Embrace freedom in Christ.

- Jesus teaches us to long for heaven. His life was a piece of heaven coming down to Earth for us. Ask Him for His will to be done on Earth as it is in heaven. Pray for His kingdom to come to Earth and write your prayer and/ or response below.

DOER OF THE WORD

How can you apply what you have heard today? (James 1:22)

A SAVIOR OR A MURDERER

PRAISE GOD. REPENT OF SIN. ASK FOR OTHERS + YOURSELF.
YIELD TO GOD. WAIT AND LISTEN.

Now at the feast he used to release for them one prisoner for whom they asked. And among the rebels in prison, who had committed murder in the insurrection, there was a man called Barabbas. And the crowd came up and began to ask Pilate to do as he usually did for them. And he answered them, saying, "Do you want me to release for you the King of the Jews?" For he perceived that it was out of envy that the chief priests had delivered him up. But the chief priests stirred up the crowd to have him release for them Barabbas instead. And Pilate again said to them, "Then what shall I do with the man you call the King of the Jews?" And they cried out again, "Crucify him." And Pilate said to them, "Why, what evil has he done?" But they shouted all the more, "Crucify him." So Pilate, wishing to satisfy the crowd, released for them Barabbas, and having scourged Jesus, he delivered him to be crucified."

Mark 15:6-15 ESV

Additional Reading: Matthew 27:15-23; Luke 23:18-15; John 18:33-40

▶ Observe the conflicts at play in this story. In Matthew, the chief priests and elders were persuading the crowd to choose Barabbas while Pilate's wife was encouraging him to have nothing to do with Jesus because of a dream she had. Pilate offers the choice as a means to gain popularity with the masses. What is the downfall of being persuaded by emotion over truth?

• Jesus' scourging was one of the most barbaric forms of punishment outside of the cross that was available during this time. Do some searching on Google or in your Bible and write below what scourging was. Get a picture of what suffering was necessary to atone for our sin. Write also your response to this sacrifice from Jesus.

▶ Read John 18:33-40. Jesus and Pilate talk before He and Barabbas are presented to the crowd. Their conversation centers around kingship. What is the nature of Jesus' kingdom? What are His followers supposed to be about?

> DOER OF THE WORD <

How can you apply what you have heard today? (James 1:22)

WEEK SEVEN

PROCLAIM HIS EXCELLENCIES

PRAISE GOD. REPENT OF SIN. ASK FOR OTHERS + YOURSELF.
YIELD TO GOD. WAIT AND LISTEN.

As you read this week, put yourself in the crowds as you learn from Jesus' words, His actions and His priorities. This is hard to read for us as we take the Savior we worship and watch Him suffer unimaginable pain on our behalf. Read this week with a heart of gratitude and thankfulness. Feel the weight of His love for you and pay attention to the words spoken against Him and the accusations thrown His way. See God's plan at work and let it move your conversations this week.

• *Read 1 Peter 2:9 and write it below.*

Write out some thoughts on each of these identity characteristics that are assigned to you as a believer.

  • *A Chosen Race:*

  • *A Royal Priesthood:*

  • *A Holy Nation:*

  • *A People for His Own:*

BLOW OUT ONE CANDLE
(YOU SHOULD HAVE 1 LIT)

Jesus lived in a way that left no doubt to those that experienced or even heard about Him as to who He worshipped. They knew who He represented and who He loved. Even at the age of 12 He would spend time with the teachers of the time as He had to be about His Father's business (Luke 2:49).

This is our example. As we just read when Jesus was praying in the garden before His betrayal, He cried out to His Father in utter despair and yet still was able to desire His Father's will for His life above His own. He actively "proclaimed His excellencies" as He taught Peter the importance of experiencing God's will even when there could be a better way in our limited understanding.

I talk often about the things I'm most passionate about. It doesn't take long for a conversation to turn from "small talk", which I feel so uncomfortable with, into something of deeper meaning and purpose. I feel myself coming alive when I get to speak on any number of topics I have experience in or find endlessly fascinating. It honestly doesn't even deter my excitement when I meet someone who couldn't care less about what I'm talking about. Yes, I have problems. Well aware of that, thank you!

Part of our comfort in sharing freely has to do with our identity. When do you feel truly at home? When do you relax internally and feel at peace in a conversation? How many conversations do you have without an agenda?

In all of our zeal and drive to tell people about Jesus and the freedom we experience through Him, I feel like at times we get away from Jesus' heart for people. What I've always found magnetic about Jesus' life is that sinners wanted to be around Him. When all of society had shut them out... the religious elite as well as the everyday common folk, Jesus was the one they found acceptance in. Jesus is the one who offered healing and hope.

▶ *Do people want to be around the Jesus you reflect or talk about?*

If we're having a hard time talking about Him or experiencing with others what He is actively working in our hearts by being in relationship with Him, shouldn't it cause some introspection on our part to figure out what identity we're living from? There is so much right about loving people without an end goal in mind. People aren't projects. Salvations are not goals to achieve. Jesus, in His mercy and love for you, at times will invite you to be a part of someone coming to know Him for the first time. What a privilege and calling! All we're asked to do is share and walk into the light that He has made available to us.

I know so many times we want to strategize and formulate this because it gives us a sense of control and fulfillment that we wouldn't get otherwise. What if we just "proclaimed His excellencies"? What would happen?

What if you reached out to the unchurched and loved them because you cared about them? What if you didn't see a rejection of your invitation to church as personal but instead asked to hear their story? I'm convinced that love becomes complicated once we introduce expectations and timelines. If we could only grasp the beauty in the inefficiency of love, I think we would grow closer to the heart of Jesus towards us and find the freedom we've been searching for in sharing the gospel with others.

DOER OF THE WORD

How can you apply what you have heard today? (James 1:22)

JUSTICE: THE UNNOTICED

PRAISE GOD. REPENT OF SIN. ASK FOR OTHERS + YOURSELF.
YIELD TO GOD. WAIT AND LISTEN.

- *Write out Micah 6:8 and then circle the three things we should do.*

The Message translates this passage, "But he's already made it plain how to live, what to do, what God is looking for in men and women. It's quite simple: Do what is fair and just to your neighbor, be compassionate and loyal in your love, And don't take yourself too seriously— take God seriously."

First, let's look at this topic internally. Where do you, <insert name here>, identify with the unnoticed? Justice is not about serving only. It's absolutely not about an "us vs. them" mentality. If these types of barriers exist in any way today or if we have a desire to serve simply out of duty or obligation, I want to connect with God's heart and see if He can't bring healing to our brokenness.

▶ *In what ways are you unnoticed today? List out 2 or 3 things that come to mind.*

Jesus, there are many ways and many times throughout my day where I think those around me have no clue what I'm going through. I pass people, I see people with my eyes without uttering a single word in their direction. I stand next to people in an elevator and wait patiently for sounds to stop so I can get off and go into my world of work. Jesus, what are you doing in our hearts and what are you teaching us in those moments? Do you notice me? Where can I go where you're not? I pray we would live daily knowing that you see us. Speak to the thoughts we refuse to share with anyone and love us in ways we don't even know how to ask others to do. Let us have compassion on those that are quiet, who are not on stage or on TV or on the sports field and see their lives and the significance of them. Let us remember those who work night shifts and on the buildings we find ourselves in and the roads we drive across and be thankful for their unseen contribution. Let us rest in your intention for us and see the value that we possess as one of Yours. We pray these things in Jesus' name. Amen.

Next, let's take this heart to those around us.

▶ *Who are people you know that are unnoticed? Write their names or initials below.*

"as we look not to the things that are seen but to the things that are unseen. For the things that are seen are transient, but the things that are unseen are eternal."

2 Corinthians 4:18 ESV

Who, in your life, needs to be seen today? What's crazy about this is it could be a complete stranger that you've never before seen before today. At the checkout counter, look them in the eye and ask them how their day is going. Invite the waitress into your meal and see the 45 minutes you will interact with her as a way to encourage her, thank her for serving you and introduce her to your family. Offer to pray for her or over her during or after your meal. Maybe offer to get groceries for the single Mom down the street who loves her kids passionately but feels she doesn't get to spend enough time with them just playing on the floor.

When you see someone cleaning the building you're in, thank them. Ask them how their day is going. This is being the hands and feet of Jesus in our world. Appreciating the nurse that chooses to spend her nights around your newborn babies so you can get a couple of hours of sleep should happen every time you take your baby from her in the hospital. Man we loved those nurses. Choose to see the widow at a wedding who is reliving past memories of her and her husband in better days. Ask questions about him. Learn from him through her descriptions.

For every person that is "noticed" in our world there are likely thousands that are not. Simple gestures can and will be remembered for years. Post it notes are great little tools for this. Grabbing a Sonic drink or a meal for someone who sits by you. Taking the middle seat on a plane so someone else can only worry about one side of their body touching another instead of two. Get creative in serving those around you. Learn to love what you don't fully understand in order to see God in ways you never knew you could.

DOER OF THE WORD

In light of what you've written, read and thought about, what is one thing you can do today to take care of the unnoticed? (James 1:22)

A BLOODY MESS

PRAISE GOD. REPENT OF SIN. ASK FOR OTHERS + YOURSELF.
YIELD TO GOD. WAIT AND LISTEN.

"Then the soldiers of the governor took Jesus into the governor's headquarters, and they gathered the whole battalion before him. And they stripped him and put a scarlet robe on him, and twisting together a crown of thorns, they put it on his head and put a reed in his right hand. And kneeling before him, they mocked him, saying, "Hail, King of the Jews!" And they spit on him and took the reed and struck him on the head. And when they had mocked him, they stripped him of the robe and put his own clothes on him and led him away to crucify him."

Matthew 27:27-31 ESV

When it says Jesus was presented in front of a whole battalion, this was anywhere from 120-600 soldiers. The mocking followed, as Roman custom would have it, as there was someone else claiming to be king in their midst. This was meant to diminish him and solidify Roman strength. The exchange between Jesus and Pilate in John 18:28-40 is especially worth reading as the scourging and mocking should be seen in the context of this conversation with Pilate. The clarity of Jesus' message in the midst of so much physical suffering is representative of His singular mission. Pilate repeatedly finds nothing worthy of death in Jesus' life but succumbs to pressure from the Israelites to crucify Him for claiming to be the Son of God.

Additional Reading: Mark 15:16-20, John 18:28-40, John 19:1-3, Isaiah 53:5-7

▶ Do some quick research on the purpose of mocking in Roman culture. List some of the differences in how Jesus exerted His authority as opposed to the Roman rulers or the Sanhedrin. Why do you believe Jesus chose this path of authority?

▶ We've read a lot in this passage about peer pressure driving action in people, whether they agree with the action they perform or not. How should Jesus' response to the mocking change our behavior when we face opposition?

▶ Read Isaiah 53:5-7. How was this scene a fulfillment of that prophecy? Keep in mind Isaiah was written anywhere from 500-700 years before Jesus' time on Earth.

DOER OF THE WORD

How can you apply what you have heard today? (James 1:22)

SABBATH: REST AND RENEW

PRAISE GOD. REPENT OF SIN. ASK FOR OTHERS + YOURSELF.
YIELD TO GOD. WAIT AND LISTEN.

Welcome to Sabbath. Today is a day of rest, reflection and restoration. I encourage you to find some quiet in your day today, get alone, pray and recharge. We practice this as followers of Jesus, emulating His ways and getting alone to rest.

After [Jesus] had dismissed [the crowds], he went up on a mountainside by himself to pray. When evening came, he was [still] there alone."

Matthew 14:23 ESV

Very early in the morning, while it was still dark, Jesus got up, left the house and went off to a solitary place, where he prayed.

Mark 1:35 ESV

Refer back to the first week's entry on Sabbath to remind yourself of the things you identified as most restful to you as well as what is helpful for you when trying to hear from God. Choose today how you'll implement one or more of these suggestions. Pay attention here to how God wired you to respond to Him. It may be unique to how others experience Him. It may be very similar. The goal is not to have a relationship with Jesus like someone else does. Learn to see your unique makeup as what leads you into deeper relationship and connection. Explore that today.

Below are some questions to ponder and respond to in order to help process what the Lord has been doing in your heart. Don't worry about looking up what you've written down in prior days and repeating those answers here. Really seek the Lord and ask Him the following:

▶ *What is one truth that has stayed with me from last week?*

▶ How would you have me apply that one truth or one lesson for this coming week?

▶ What do you think of me? What do you think of my heart?

Come back and journal here about your day before you go to sleep.

▶ What did you learn about God on your Sabbath?

▶ What did you learn about yourself?

▶ What do you need to do or not do next time to make for a more holy Sabbath?

▶ Anything else you learned or realized or noticed today?

> DOER OF THE WORD <

How can you apply what you have heard today? (James 1:22)

FORSAKEN

PRAISE GOD. REPENT OF SIN. ASK FOR OTHERS + YOURSELF.
YIELD TO GOD. WAIT AND LISTEN.

"And they compelled a passerby, Simon of Cyrene, who was coming in from the country, the father of Alexander and Rufus, to carry his cross. And they brought him to the place called Golgotha (which means Place of a Skull). And they offered him wine mixed with myrrh, but he did not take it. And they crucified him and divided his garments among them, casting lots for them, to decide what each should take. And it was the third hour when they crucified him. And the inscription of the charge against him read, "The King of the Jews." And with him they crucified two robbers, one on his right and one on his left.

And those who passed by derided him, wagging their heads and saying, "Aha! You who would destroy the temple and rebuild it in three days, save yourself, and come down from the cross!" So also the chief priests with the scribes mocked him to one another, saying, "He saved others; he cannot save himself. Let the Christ, the King of Israel, come down now from the cross that we may see and believe." Those who were crucified with him also reviled him.

And when the sixth hour had come, there was darkness over the whole land until the ninth hour. And at the ninth hour Jesus cried with a loud voice, "Eloi, Eloi, lema sabachthani?" which means, "My God, my God, why have you forsaken me?" And some of the bystanders hearing it said, "Behold, he is calling Elijah." And someone ran and filled a sponge with sour wine, put it on a reed and gave it to him to drink, saying, "Wait, let us see whether Elijah will come to take him down." And Jesus uttered a loud cry and breathed his last. And the curtain of the temple was torn in two, from top to bottom. And when the centurion, who stood facing him, saw that in this way he breathed his last, he said, "Truly this man was the Son of God!""

Mark 15:21-27, 29-39 ESV

Additional Reading: Matthew 27:32-56, Luke 23:26-49, John 19:17-37, Psalm 22, Romans 3:23-26, 2 Corinthians 5:21

▶ Read Matthew 27:51-55. What was the centurion's reaction to Jesus' death? What events do you think were most effective in leading him to this conclusion?

▶ How does Psalm 22 (written nearly 1,000 years prior to this event), which is a roadmap of the suffering and verbal responses to it by an innocent person, reflect the crucifixion story? Write down any parallels between the two that you observe.

▶ What were Jesus' final words? What will you remember the most after reading the crucifixion account from all of the gospels?

DOER OF THE WORD

How can you apply what you have heard today? (James 1:22)

PRAYER: ENGAGE AND ENJOY

PRAISE GOD. REPENT OF SIN. ASK FOR OTHERS + YOURSELF.
YIELD TO GOD. WAIT AND LISTEN.

Today will be all about prayer. Prayer can take on many forms, but at its heart it is connecting with the heart of God through praising, asking, repenting and responding to His will for your life. It can be done while on your knees in a worshipful posture with your head down, while walking/running down the street, through singing with arms raised or through quiet solitude alone. So challenge yourself during these days to pray in different ways to explore the depths of your relationship with the Lord.

If the questions below are helpful for you, please use them as a guide during this time today. If you feel strongly led to engage with God in a different way that's more meaningful or personal this week, please use this time for that. While the questions and ways of praying will be the same each week, I can guarantee the actual words used, words received from God, thoughts and experiences of forgiveness, love, confusion, pain, etc. will be very different from week to week. Use the truths that you've learned in your study time and lean on the Scripture and promises that have been discovered.

Engage your heart. Enjoy the process and connection with your Creator.

• *Jesus, I want to glorify and praise you today for...*

• *This week I've felt compelled to go deeper in this area:_____*

▶ *I pray today that you would speak to me concerning my area of deepest need. What would you have to say to me today?*

BLOW OUT ONE CANDLE
(YOU SHOULD HAVE NONE LIT)

- Lord, this week I want to confess to you where I've been most convicted. Write below where you feel God challenging you the most. This will be hard but fight for your heart in this process and be honest about where He is gently but firmly bringing His purposes to light in your life. Repent from sin. Embrace freedom in Christ.

- Jesus teaches us to long for heaven. His life was a piece of heaven coming down to Earth for us. Ask Him for His will to be done on Earth as it is in heaven. Pray for His kingdom to come to Earth and write your prayer and/or response below.

DOER OF THE WORD

How can you apply what you have heard today? (James 1:22)

DEAD AND BURIED

PRAISE GOD. REPENT OF SIN. ASK FOR OTHERS + YOURSELF.
YIELD TO GOD. WAIT AND LISTEN.

"Now there was a man named Joseph, from the Jewish town of Arimathea. He was
a member of the council, a good and righteous man, who had not consented to
their decision and action; and he was looking for the kingdom of God. This man
went to Pilate and asked for the body of Jesus. Then he took it down and wrapped
it in a linen shroud and laid him in a tomb cut in stone, where no one had ever
yet been laid. It was the day of Preparation, and the Sabbath was beginning. The
women who had come with him from Galilee followed and saw the tomb and how
his body was laid. Then they returned and prepared spices and ointments. On the
Sabbath they rested according to the commandment."

Luke 23:50-56 ESV

"The next day, that is, after the day of Preparation, the chief priests and the
Pharisees gathered before Pilate and said, "Sir, we remember how that impostor
said, while he was still alive, 'After three days I will rise.' Therefore order the tomb
to be made secure until the third day, lest his disciples go and steal him away and
tell the people, 'He has risen from the dead,' and the last fraud will be worse than
the first." Pilate said to them, "You have a guard of soldiers. Go, make it as secure
as you can." So they went and made the tomb secure by sealing the stone and
setting a guard."

Matthew 27:62-66 ESV

Additional Reading: Matthew 27:57-61, Mark 15:42-47, John 19:38-42, Isaiah 53:9

▶ The account of Joseph of Arimathea is relevant to us today as it's one of the first, if not the first account of a believers actions after Jesus' life. What can you apply to your life today in light of Joseph's devotion to Jesus?

▶ What is the significance in identifying a stone that had to be rolled over the entrance of the tomb?

▶ Observe the faithfulness of the women in this account. How does it encourage your faith in Jesus, especially during seemingly hopeless times?

DOER OF THE WORD

How can you apply what you have heard today? (James 1:22)

WEEK EIGHT

HE IS ALIVE!

PRAISE GOD. REPENT OF SIN. ASK FOR OTHERS + YOURSELF.
YIELD TO GOD. WAIT AND LISTEN.

As we close this study on the final days of Jesus, I wanted to spend this last day getting as close to the experience of Jesus' resurrection as possible. Our only way to do this is to immerse ourselves in His word and read eyewitness accounts from His followers. Each gospel has different levels of detail while some include stories that others do not.

We're going to read through John's account and discuss here with commentary and questions, but let me encourage you to read the other accounts as well in **Matthew 28, Mark 16, and Luke 24.** Also watching Passion of the Christ on this day can hold special significance as you see these words transform from the page to the large screen.

Just know that what you celebrate today and experience is the very foundation of our faith. The fact that Jesus rose from the dead to conquer sin once and for all on our behalf and provide final atonement for the sin we find ourselves entrapped in daily brings a light and hope to our lives that otherwise would be impossible.

So celebrate today and thank God for the gift of Jesus! See the reactions of the people He appeared to and put yourself in their shoes for a moment. Feel your heart burn within you along with the men on the road to Emmaus as Jesus revealed the entirety of Scripture to them and how it pointed to Himself the whole time. See the joy in Mary as she recognizes Him for the first time and feel the excitement of the disciples as they encounter Jesus behind locked doors. *This is hope personified. This is who we worship and devote our lives to. He is worthy of our praise.*

"Now on the first day of the week Mary Magdalene came to the tomb early, while it was still dark, and saw that the stone had been taken away from the tomb. So she ran and went to Simon Peter and the other disciple, the one whom Jesus loved, and said to them, "They have taken the Lord out of the tomb, and we do not know where they have laid him."

So Peter went out with the other disciple, and they were going toward the tomb. Both of them were running together, but the other disciple outran Peter and reached the tomb first. And stooping to look in, he saw the linen cloths lying there, but he did not go in. Then Simon Peter came, following him, and went into the tomb.

He saw the linen cloths lying there, and the face cloth, which had been on Jesus' head, not lying with the linen cloths but folded up in a place by itself. Then the other disciple, who had reached the tomb first, also went in, and he saw and believed; for as yet they did not understand the Scripture, that he must rise from the dead. Then the disciples went back to their homes."

John 20:1-10 ESV

I picture Mary and the disciples here being caught up in the moment. Their first expectation in the morning was clearly not to find an empty tomb. Yes Jesus had taught them this and it was common knowledge as the guards over the tomb would not have been necessary if Jesus rising on the third day was only something the disciples knew.

Seeing them act utterly shocked and in disbelief is refreshing. This makes them relatable. These are people like us. John points out not once but twice how he beat Peter to the grave while running. On the most significant day in history, one of the writers of the gospels is playing a silly competitive game just like we would. And these are the ones Jesus is telling us His story through. He uses us all.

"But Mary stood weeping outside the tomb, and as she wept she stooped to look into the tomb. And she saw two angels in white, sitting where the body of Jesus had lain, one at the head and one at the feet. They said to her, "Woman, why are you weeping?" She said to them, "They have taken away my Lord, and I do not know where they have laid him."

Having said this, she turned around and saw Jesus standing, but she did not know that it was Jesus. Jesus said to her, "Woman, why are you weeping? Whom are you seeking?" Supposing him to be the gardener, she said to him, "Sir, if you have carried him away, tell me where you have laid him, and I will take him away." Jesus said to her, "Mary." She turned and said to him in Aramaic, "Rabboni!" (which means Teacher). Jesus said to her, "Do not cling to me, for I have not yet ascended to the Father; but go to my brothers and say to them, 'I am ascending to my Father and your Father, to my God and your God.'" Mary Magdalene went and announced to the disciples, "I have seen the Lord"—and that he had said these things to her."

John 20:11-18 ESV

Mary wasn't just crying. It says here she was weeping. When she turns around to talk to what she perceives to be the gardener, she has no time to entertain his question as to the cause of her emotion. She has one focus and one focus only. Where is my Lord? In times of uncertainty or deep stress, our search for the Lord should be relentless and focused. We should have a burning need to be around Him and should stop at nothing to get to Him.

When Jesus chooses to reveal Himself to her, he uses a single word. "Mary". I love this. There are examples throughout Scripture on the significance of names and the fact that God knows each of ours. This truth should not be dismissed. He has a purpose for our lives. He teaches others through them. If it wasn't for Mary, who would've announced Jesus' return to the disciples? You have a calling on your life and a purpose to fulfill. Let your devotion to Christ reveal this in time and learn to respond as Mary did, without hesitation and with total obedience.

"On the evening of that day, the first day of the week, the doors being locked where the disciples were for fear of the Jews, Jesus came and stood among them and said to them, "Peace be with you." When he had said this, he showed them his hands and his side. Then the disciples were glad when they saw the Lord. Jesus said to them again, "Peace be with you. As the Father has sent me, even so I am sending you." And when he had said this, he breathed on them and said to them, "Receive the Holy Spirit. If you forgive the sins of any, they are forgiven them; if you withhold forgiveness from any, it is withheld.""

John 20:19-23 ESV

Jesus first reaffirms their faith in Him by appearing and second equips them for the work that will define the rest of their lives. His message to Mary to "not cling to me" makes more sense as we read this passage because in order to carry out the work, Jesus gives us the Holy Spirit. What we do for the kingdom of God during our time on Earth is not possible without the Holy Spirit's influence. Working in our own strength leads to burnout and ineffectiveness. Embrace the authority you have been given as a disciple/follower of Jesus. He has equipped you for eternal work in the lives of people you encounter.

"Now Thomas, one of the Twelve, called the Twin, was not with them when Jesus came. So the other disciples told him, "We have seen the Lord." But he said to them, "Unless I see in his hands the mark of the nails, and place my finger into the mark of the nails, and place my hand into his side, I will never believe."

Eight days later, his disciples were inside again, and Thomas was with them. Although the doors were locked, Jesus came and stood among them and said, "Peace be with you."

Then he said to Thomas, "Put your finger here, and see my hands; and put out your hand, and place it in my side. Do not disbelieve, but believe." Thomas answered him, "My Lord and my God!" Jesus said to him, "Have you believed because you have seen me? Blessed are those who have not seen and yet have believed.""

John 20:24-29 ESV

Thomas' doubts were real. We don't have much background on his life to help bring context to this moment or the reasons why he seemed to be given over to doubt more easily than the others, but nevertheless Jesus chose to address it. He appeared first to the 10 disciples and then 8 days later to the 11, including Thomas.

Jesus gives Thomas the opportunity to see Himself so that His unbelief would not prevail. He also says how blessed those of us are who have not seen and still believe. We fall in the second category. Some of us have a truly difficult time getting past this unbelief. My encouragement for you from this text is that you shouldn't ignore it. It's not something to be ashamed of.

What's important is that Thomas did not see his doubts as the definitive truth he would believe for the rest of his life. He showed up eight days later. He displayed the courage to doubt his doubts. He kept searching. He was teachable. He was humble in allowing himself to be wrong. Jesus captured his heart as a result. Instead of Thomas' faith being shaken, it was restored.

"You are the light of the world. A city set on a hill cannot be hidden. Nor do people light a lamp and put it under a basket, but on a stand, and it gives light to all in the house. In the same way, let your light shine before others, so that they may see your good works and give glory to your Father who is in heaven."

Matthew 5:14-16 ESV

Taking a passage from Jesus' Sermon on the Mount, I wanted us to read this as an identity verse for us to get in touch with who God created us to be. You, believer, are the light of the world. You should not hide your true self, your true nature or your true beliefs from anyone. You being you will bring light to a dark world because you reflect the love of Jesus with the way you live your life. Be known to people of this world. Don't let comfort be your ultimate guide. Let your deeds, your service and your desires turn people's attention to your Creator, who placed the very capacity for these things in you from the very beginning.

Jesus has said you will do greater things than He when equipped with the power of the Holy Spirit. Change your world today and glorify your Father in the process. He has risen for this.

▶ What is the message of the empty tomb? What does it mean for you?

DOER OF THE WORD

How can you apply what you have heard today? (James 1:22)